I'M JUST SAYIN'!

KIM ZIMMER

WITH LAURA MORTON

I'M JUST SAYIN'!

3 Deaths, 7 Husbands, and a Clone!
My Life as a Daytime Diva

NEW AMERICAN LIBRARY

NEW AMERICAN LIBRARY
Published by New American Library, a division of
Penguin Group (USA) Inc., 375 Hudson Street,
New York, New York 10014, USA
Penguin Group (Canada), 90 Eglinton Avenue East, Suite 700, Toronto,
Ontario M4P 2Y3, Canada (a division of Pearson Penguin Canada Inc.)
Penguin Books Ltd., 80 Strand, London WC2R 0RL, England
Penguin Ireland, 25 St. Stephen's Green, Dublin 2,
Ireland (a division of Penguin Books Ltd.)
Penguin Group (Australia), 250 Camberwell Road, Camberwell, Victoria 3124,
Australia (a division of Pearson Australia Group Pty. Ltd.)
Penguin Books India Pvt. Ltd., 11 Community Centre, Panchsheel Park,
New Delhi - 110 017, India
Penguin Group (NZ), 67 Apollo Drive, Rosedale, Auckland 0632,
New Zealand (a division of Pearson New Zealand Ltd.)
Penguin Books (South Africa) (Pty.) Ltd., 24 Sturdee Avenue,
Rosebank, Johannesburg 2196, South Africa

Penguin Books Ltd., Registered Offices:
80 Strand, London WC2R 0RL, England

First published by New American Library,
a division of Penguin Group (USA) Inc.

First Printing, August 2011
10 9 8 7 6 5 4 3 2 1

REGISTERED TRADEMARK—MARCA REGISTRADA

LIBRARY OF CONGRESS CATALOGING-IN-PUBLICATION DATA:
Zimmer, Kim.
   I'm just sayin'!: three deaths, seven husbands and a clone!:my life as a daytime diva/Kim Zimmer
with Laura Morton.
      p.   cm.
   ISBN 978-0-451-23343-1
   1. Zimmer, Kim. 2. Actors—United States—Biography. I. Morton, Laura. II. Title.
   PN2287.Z565A3   2011
   791.4502'.8092—dc22   2011005351
   [B]

Set in Sabon LT STD
Designed by Alissa Amell

Printed in the United States of America

PUBLISHER'S NOTE
   Penguin is committed to publishing works of quality and integrity. In that spirit, we are proud to
offer this book to our readers; however the story, the experiences and the words are the authors alone.
   While the author has made every effort to provide accurate telephone numbers and Internet ad-
dresses at the time of publication, neither the publisher nor the author assumes any responsibility for
errors, or for changes that occur after publication. Further, publisher does not have any control over
and does not assume any responsibility for author or third-party Web sites or their content.

Courtesy of the Zimmer Family Archives

My mother's favorite song was "Memory" from the Broadway musical *Cats*. She loved to make memories, so in her honor, and with love and appreciation to my dad, Jack; my sister, Karen; my husband, A.C.; and my beautiful children, Rachel, Max and Jake, I dedicate this book.

CONTENTS

CONTENTS

Dear Friend,

I thought many times about writing a firsthand account of life as a "daytime diva," but, as with many things, procrastination set in and my schedule was substantially full and eventually the desire faded. However, all that changed on the morning it was announced that Guiding Light, *the oldest show in broadcast history, was being canceled after a seventy-two-year run!*

Writing this book was so therapeutic for me. It gave me the chance to really contemplate my years spent playing Reva Shayne. It also gave me the opportunity to put a period on this chapter of my life so that I could start anew. That might sound easy, but after twenty-six years playing the same part, it was anything but!

I wanted to have something that I could share with the lifelong and devoted followers of Guiding Light. *You are the generations of viewers who got to share our stories with us. There were times when I was honored to meet as many as four, or occasionally even more, generations of viewers at an event, all of whom were so proud to tell me about passing this show down from generation to generation within their family! I was a fan of the show too, and as you will read, just as hurt and confused by its cancellation as everyone else. Writing this story has given me the chance to revisit in my heart the many times I got to meet you, the fans, who are really the people responsible for keeping this show on the air for seventy-two glorious years! We are going to take a peek behind the curtain and get a real bird's-eye view of what my life was really like on the set, and off.*

Many very talented actors got their start on Guiding Light *and went on to make amazing careers for themselves. Among them are Kevin Bacon, Allison Janney* (The West Wing), *Melina Kanakaredes* (CSI:NY), *Emmy winner Tammy Blanchard, Tony nominee Laura Bell Bundy, Billy Dee Williams, JoBeth Williams, Ian Ziering* (Beverly Hills, 90210), *Nia Long, Taye Diggs, Victor Garber . . . and many, many more.*

And a lot of good actors came there and stayed. Michael Zaslow was the best villain ever on soaps until the producers fired him when he was in the early stages of ALS, after he'd played Roger Thorpe on and off for twenty-five years. Jordan Clarke played a gynecologist on Guiding Light *several years before taking on the role of Billy Lewis, whom he ultimately portrayed for twenty-five years! Frank Dicopoulos was another quarter-century man. And Tina Sloan held the record for the longest continuing character on* Guiding Light *when the show went off the air.*

And then there were all of the actors who started on the show as young adults, left for a number of years, and then returned to the show later, including Michael O'Leary, Grant Aleksander, Robert Newman, and yes, even me.

It was the cancellation of Guiding Light *that finally motivated me to drive to my local Staples and purchase a stack of legal pads so I could begin the process of put-*

ting all of my thoughts, memories, and emotions on paper. My brain was flooded with fond memories of my years at Guiding Light, *but those were quickly overshadowed by my sadness, which then turned toward anger and frustration, as you might expect after such a heavy and unexpected blow.*

How did the powers that be allow this to happen? *I found myself spewing venom with my mighty pen about this event I had no control over, and as cathartic and therapeutic as it was for me to write, it was way too angry to be enjoyable or amusing to a reader. Oh, yeah, I wrote some letters that, looking back, I am really, really happy I never sent. Still, it felt good to get it all out, even if mine was the only set of eyes to ever read what I had to say.*

As I continued to write, however, something wonderful happened. My bitterness and anger began to give way to thoughtful and meaningful reflection. That mental shift started me down a whole new path—one where I could look back and revisit the absolutely amazing journey I've had throughout my life.

The purpose of this book isn't to take you through a step-by-step account of my life, but instead to give you a chance to walk with me as we revisit the ups and downs, the highs and lows, the peaks and valleys that I've experienced both on-screen and off. Together, we'll chronicle the career of this ol' gal from Grand Rapids, Michigan, who was lucky enough to snag the greatest role in the history of a daytime serial drama!

At least, I think it was the greatest.

And there are about 1.7 million others, maybe even you, who I'm sure would agree!

I have spent a large portion of my professional career as Reva, and in those years I've gathered many stories I think you'll enjoy. When you spend as much time together as the cast and crew of Guiding Light *did, you experience it all: the good, the bad, and the ugly!*

So it's with great pride and appreciation that I present this book to all of you who stuck with us through thick and thin, eighteen presidents, five major wars, innumerable marriages, divorces, births, deaths, and so much more. My admiration and appreciation for all of you is endless! Please enjoy this fanciful and thoughtful journey through the parallel lives of Kim Zimmer and Reva Shayne!

Love,
Kim

I'M JUST SAYIN'!

I woke up on a cold concrete slab with no idea of where I was
or why. The glaring starkness of the room was blinding. I
struggled to focus my eyes through the horrific nonstop pounding in my head. When I finally sat up and got my bearings, I
noticed what appeared to be a one-armed hooker sitting on the
same concrete slab staring back at me.

"What are you in for, honey?" she asked.

In for?

What was she talking about?

And why didn't I know my next line? I have never forgotten
a single word in any of my scripts, but this time, I had no idea
where to go with this scene. I was blank and confused but,
strangely, not panicked.

My professional integrity and experience allowed me to patiently wait for the director to call, "Cut," but his command
never came. When I looked above me, I began wondering why
the usual and familiar theatrical stage lighting was absent, and
why there were only harsh flickering tubes of fluorescent lights
overhead. The one thing I knew for sure was that no one looked
good in lighting that severe. I was certain someone had made a
horrible mistake.

"Where are the director and the rest of the crew?" I asked the hooker, who, remarkably, remained in perfect character. She looked at me like *I* was crazy and never uttered a single word.

"Someone yell, 'Cut'!" I shouted.

An officer peered through the thick iron bars. "Quiet, Zimmer, or I'll take you to isolation."

Wait a minute.

Did she say Zimmer?

My character is Reva Shayne-Lewis-Lewis-Spaulding-Lewis-Winslow-Cooper-Lewis-Lewis-O'Neill.

Not a Zimmer in there.

What had I done?

I knew Reva had been arrested plenty of times.

There was the incident in New Orleans when she was falsely accused and jailed for being a spy by Confederate General Hudson during a time-traveling incident in 2001.

And then there was the time she practiced medicine without a license on an injured Cain Harris.

She accidentally hit Dylan Lewis with her car, and she found out much later he was really the son she'd given up for adoption years ago!

She stole a car from a used-car dealership in the Florida Keys, and then drove it off the nearest bridge.

She chloroformed Annie Dutton and then kidnapped her.

And she was falsely accused of murdering Annie's stillborn baby.

Yes, Reva had been accused of many crimes over the years.

But this time, it wasn't Reva sitting in a jail cell.

Nope.

It was me.

I had spent a wonderful evening in Los Angeles eating sushi with a dear friend whom I hadn't seen for months. She brought along three bottles of wine from her very own vineyard! The two of us sat eating sashimi, avoiding any carbs other than those found in our wineglasses. We laughed about old times for hours before saying our good-byes that chilly January night.

I hopped into the shiny black pickup truck I had borrowed from my son while I was in town for pilot season. I buckled up, checked my mirrors, pushed my hair back, and put the truck into drive.

It didn't take long for me to realize I was lost as I headed onto the local freeway. Los Angeles isn't my home. I have spent lots of time there throughout my career, but I have happily called Montclair, New Jersey, home for more than twenty years. Even though I sort of know my way around L.A., it's relatively easy to get turned around on the freeways, and even easier after having a few drinks.

Panic swept through my body as I caught that dreaded glimpse of flashing red and blue lights in my rearview mirror that night. The cops were going to pull me over, and there was no way to fake being sober. I knew I'd had too much to drink. I knew I should never have gotten in my car to drive that night. I knew I was fucked when I heard a loud voice over the patrol car speaker commanding me to pull over.

"Could you step out of the car, ma'am?" The officer wasn't really asking. It was more of a demand.

"Have you been drinking?" he asked, though I am sure he already knew the answer. There was really no point in lying to a policeman in this type of situation, so I confessed that I had thrown back a few glasses of wine at dinner that night.

Next, the cop told me he needed a female officer present to continue. I wasn't sure what would happen next. I was actually yukking it up with the police, thinking I might be able to disarm them. Unfortunately, one of the two cops was a rookie who was being trained, so he was doing everything by the book. There was no room for humor or lightheartedness. I was drunk and knew there was no fighting what was about to happen. They really put me through the paces after the female cop arrived, conducting every field sobriety test you've seen on *Cops*. I was wearing three-inch heels that night and asked to take them off before I did the tests so I'd have a better shot at passing, but I was too drunk for it to make a difference. Even barefoot I failed, and was immediately arrested on suspicion of driving under the influence of alcohol. I was handcuffed and carted off to jail in the backseat of their patrol car.

To be very honest, this wasn't the first time I had chosen to get behind the wheel after having a few drinks, but clearly my number was up. This was the one time I got caught. I was embarrassed and scared, but did my best to defuse what was about to become a truly unforgettable experience.

I don't think the officers recognized me, and if they did, they surely didn't give a damn. This was Hollywood. Busting a celebrity wasn't rare. I guess I wasn't a big enough star, or they just didn't watch soap operas during the day, which actually worked to my advantage. To them, I was just another blond-haired, blue-eyed drunk who was out of her element. I was treated like any average citizen who breaks the law. Looking back, I realize now that there were moments from that night I don't remember, but the ones I do are vivid. When the tow truck arrived, I was confused about why they were taking my son's car away. When I asked, the cops wouldn't answer. I got surprisingly choked up when I saw the taillights fade in the distance as the tow truck went one direction and we went in another.

I was taken to the police station, where they confiscated my cell phone and all of my other personal possessions, something I didn't remember their doing until the next day. I was finger-printed, photographed, and then officially booked. You don't get photo approval of the mug shot, and even if you did, it's proba-bly better that they don't show you the picture. I am absolutely certain it wasn't a pretty sight.

The booking officer gave me my opportunity to make that "one phone call," which would have been great if I had known anyone's number. When they took my cell phone, they took all of my phone numbers. No one I know commits those to memory much anymore. Here's a bit of friendly advice: If you plan on breaking the law, make sure you know at least three friends' phone numbers by heart! It could very well save you from a night in jail.

My husband was back in New Jersey and it was already ter-ribly late—not to mention three hours later where he was. I didn't want to wake him; besides, I was too mortified to explain where I was.

I spent ten hours in my austere cell, surrounded by white cinder block on every side and one very impersonal toilet. The officer on duty offered me a disgusting egg-and-sausage sand-wich— at least, that's what I think it was. I couldn't eat it any-

awoke to another cold and rainy spring morning. It was the first day of April 2009, April Fools' Day, to be exact. I had a late call for work that day. I didn't have to be at *Guiding Light*'s location in Peapack, New Jersey, where we often shot the show in the last couple of years, until ten a.m.

What a luxury!

My usual morning ritual was to rise at six thirty a.m., tinkle, brush my teeth, wash my face, and apply various tightening serums (they're a miracle, right?), then head downstairs to the hissing sound coming from the cappuccino machine as my husband, A.C., cranks out my morning dose of caffeine. With a fresh, steaming hot mug of coffee in hand, I then walked to the end of the driveway and retrieved the morning paper so I could be up-to-date with my sports scores for the day. After all, our crew counted on me to defend my New York Jets during football season. Then it was on to the daily crossword puzzle to engage and challenge my brain.

The beautiful thing about my job as an actress is that I can basically roll out of bed and go straight to work without worrying about how I look. There's no need for makeup or to decide on an outfit to wear, because all of those decisions will be handled at the studio. Usually, I head out in a pair of sweatpants and a T-shirt. I might run a brush through my hair, depending on whether I'm stopping off at Starbucks or Dunkin' Donuts for a road coffee; otherwise I'm a pretty low-maintenance kinda gal who's gotten used to putting myself at the mercy of the show's crack makeup, hair, and wardrobe departments after I arrive at work!

On this particular morning, I was running a little late because the newest addition to our family, our sixty-pound pit bull/boxer–mix puppy, Emma, had jumped on my face and bathed me with licks and kisses. It took me forever to pry her off of me so I could get out the door. I figured I could blame my tardiness on the inclement weather if I had to, as it was pouring rain outside.

I'm usually a very punctual person who doesn't like being late to anything. I've always detested people who can't seem to make it to work on time. But lately, I just hadn't cared one way or the other if I rolled in a few minutes past my call time. So much drama had been building that going to work was no longer fun.

As soon as I got into my car for the thirty-five-minute drive to Peapack, my cellular phone rang.

"Hey, Kim." It was Bradley Cole, my *Guiding Light* husband number eight. Or was it nine?

"Sorry. I know I'm late. Are they already up to our scenes?" I asked him.

"No, it's not that," Brad responded. "Has anyone called you from the studio yet?"

"No," I answered. "Why?"

He took a deep breath. I knew whatever was coming next couldn't be good. "Well, um, it looks like the show's been canceled."

"Which show?" I asked, even though I already knew the answer. "*Our* show?"

"Yes!" he blurted. "Someone from the New York set just called and said the suits had already made the announcement there and were on their way to Peapack right now to make the official announcement to us!" *The suits* was what most of the actors called the people from Procter & Gamble, the sponsors and owners of our show.

"Okay," I managed to say before choking up. "I'm on my way."

Canceled?

I put the key in the ignition.

Canceled?

I turned on the defroster and windshield wipers.

Canceled?

I put my car in reverse and backed down the driveway. It's a good thing my Toyota 4Runner knew the trip to work by heart, because I was in complete shock. My mind was on full autopilot as I drove to the set that day. I skipped the usual stop for coffee because I wanted to get to Peapack in time to see the faces of the people announcing the catastrophic news to cast and crew, my other family, that they were canceling the oldest show in broadcast history!

That it was done!

Kaput!

Happy April Fools' Day, right?

All I could think was, They're *the fools!*

As I drove to the set, my mind flashed through all of the memories of my life and years on *Guiding Light*. The feeling was kind of like what I've heard people say happens when you have a near-death experience. I saw vivid and memorable scenes from the show for the entire drive. I saw images of Josh and Reva's outdoor wedding, all the fun Bradley Cole and I had shooting together in Puerto Rico, my famous fountain scene where I baptized myself the "Slut of Springfield," and so many more highlights of the years I spent playing Reva.

As I got closer to Peapack, I thought about how this news was going to affect so many people who had given their hearts to this show. I called A.C. from my car to relate the bad news. He said he wasn't surprised. In fact, he had been expecting this call for a few years, at the very least since the new regime took over in 2004.

There had been no formal discussions of cancellation, but when a show went from being one of the best and most beautifully produced daytime dramas on the air to becoming the cheapest-looking—due to wardrobe cuts, poor lighting, disappearing sets, and actors leaving when their salaries were cut— you had to believe the end was imminent. We all tried so hard to stay optimistic, but there were days when we had to dig deep to find something positive to concentrate on. The reassurance we were all looking for usually came in the form of an embrace from a cast mate or crew member—lovely, but not promising when it came to the life expectancy of the show.

After we hung up, I spent the rest of my commute to work lost in the sound of the driving rain against my windshield. I was shocked and I was angry, but then I was completely caught off guard by a sudden and unexpected feeling that came over me: relief.

For the first time in as long as I could remember, a huge weight had been lifted off my shoulders! I'd spent so many years worried about the show, and now I could let go of all of my fear and nervous apprehension. From this day forward, all I had to do was ride the wave to the bitter end.

I usually had to park across the street from the production house, where a van picked me up and shuttled me up to the set. No one was allowed to park at the house because the traffic would make the driveway too congested. That morning, I said, "Fuck it!" and drove up the driveway. What were they going to do, *fire* me?

As I pulled up in front of the show house, through the fog that had now fallen over the set, I could see Jan Conklin, one of the producers of the show, standing in the rain in tears. She was holding an umbrella, waiting for me to arrive. I got out of my car and we hugged.

"I'm so sorry, Kim," she kept saying over and over. "It's just terrible. I feel so bad for you."

This young producer had nothing to do with the show's demise. She was new to the business. I had been around the block a time or two. I assured Jan that I knew that none of this was her fault. I explained to her that I should be the one comforting her and the rest of my *Guiding Light* family. After all, I'm Mama Kim!

I walked inside to a room in the house that had been converted to the Cedars Hospital cafeteria to find everyone huddled together awaiting the official news of our cancellation. It was the largest room in the house, but we were all squeezed in there waiting for the suits to arrive.

I found a place to sit down and looked around the room at the faces of the men and women whom I'd worked so hard with five days a week, fifty weeks a year, year after year, who not only made *Guiding Light* breathe but, for many, come to life. Their expressions were a combination of shock, confusion, anger, loss, and, oddly, hope—hope that perhaps this was all some ill-fated joke. I guess I too was hoping the entire thing was someone's idea of the worst prank ever. But nobody was stepping up to scream, *April Fools'! We've actually been renewed for another three years!*

And no one was laughing. There wasn't even a joke flying around about the irony of the date. I'm sure the suits were as embarrassed to deliver the news that day as we were mortified to hear it. I was later told that April first was the last day they could either choose to pick up more episodes or make the announcement to end the show. The date was ironic, but not malicious. There was no cruel intention, although I firmly believe that someone could have made the announcement the day before to avoid the obvious lack of sensitivity.

Even though the room was full, no one was talking. The atmosphere was quiet and pretty much filled with doom and gloom. It took me a moment to notice that I was sitting next to Tony Girolami, our senior lighting designer. That was when it dawned on me that once the show went off the air, I might never see his face again! There were so many people in that room I considered family whom I probably would never see again once we taped our final episode. For the first time since my phone rang some forty minutes before, I suddenly felt my heart start to break.

When Brian Cahill and Pat Gentile, a.k.a. "the suits," finally arrived, they were with our executive producer, Ellen Wheeler. Brian was a representative from TeleNext, the company that oversaw the production of *Guiding Light* for Procter & Gamble. Everything that happened, good or bad, was at their discretion and whim. TeleNext ran the show while Procter & Gamble paid the bills. Pat was the head of Procter & Gamble Productions. He was more of a detergent man than a soap guy, if you know what I mean.

Soaps had been good for Procter & Gamble over the years because they allowed them to sell their products during the commercial breaks. They took great pride in the production of that hour of television, until about 2000, when things started to change.

There was a time when daytime television was so profitable, it paid for nighttime programming. The profits generated from soaps gave the networks the ability to produce one-hour dramas that aired in the evening, and that shot a single episode over the course of ten days. Daytime was the workhorse that provided the steady income for the networks.

But I think by 2000, so many viewers were recording the soaps, which gave them the option to fast-forward through the commercials instead of being forced to watch them like they used to, that the value of that commercial time decreased— meaning sponsors paid less for the once-coveted slots. When this happened, CBS's licensing fee went up, so producing *Guiding Light* was no longer profitable for Procter & Gamble. Their response was to keep the show going on a lower budget. They cut the funds they once allocated to production and started making *Guiding Light* cheaper and cheaper until it began to show.

We really hadn't had anyone from Procter & Gamble who took a vested interest in our show since the 1980s, when I first arrived to play Reva. Our suits then were Bob Wehling and Ed Trach, two swell guys. To be fair, Brian and Pat were nice enough, but they were all about the bottom line. Their sole purpose was to analyze and assess whether or not *Guiding Light* was still a viable property.

Ellen began with an explanation of why CBS had decided to stop airing *Guiding Light*. She had a tendency to be emotional; I had seen her moved to tears many times since she came on board in 2004. After all, she was once an actress herself. But this morning was different. Perhaps as a result of being in shock, Ellen was completely emotionless. She never shed a single tear. She was extremely composed as she spoke very briefly and to the point.

"It's true," she said. "We just got word this morning that the show has been canceled. September eighteenth, 2009, will be our last airdate. Our last workday will be around August eleventh. We are still working out the details and will keep you informed."

I thought Ellen handled the announcement with dignity, but I certainly wouldn't have wanted to be in her shoes that morning. I want to believe her lack of expression was out of respect to all of us who hadn't seen it coming. Even though she had already given the same news to the studio in New York, she'd had an hour drive to Peapack with only her thoughts and the suits by her side. Maybe she thought it would be better to just deliver the news without tying it to any personal emotion.

After giving all those gathered a rundown of the nuts and bolts of the decision to cancel the show, Ellen turned it over to

Brian Cahill, who expressed his sympathy and proceeded to tell us that the company would do everything in its power to find the show a new home. He assured all of us that this was not the end for *Guiding Light*. It was only the end with CBS.

Pat didn't have a lot to say after Ellen and Brian spoke. Pat is a kind and lovely man who didn't have to make the trip from Procter & Gamble headquarters in Cincinnati to face us. I totally believe he felt bad about the decision, but he is a businessman who had to make a choice that he felt was best for the company. He didn't factor in the fans or all of us who were now among the throngs of the unemployed.

There were a lot of tears when the suits finished speaking. The shock of our cancellation was beginning to sink in. I had to figure out what the future would hold for me, and fast! Except for Marcy Rylan, who was fully pregnant and in the glow of future motherhood, the rest of us were facing uncertain futures. We had just hired a young actor to his first daytime contract with the hope of three years of steady employment; he had been on the job only a couple of weeks when he got the news! And it was not just the actors who would be affected by this decision, but also the entire crew and production staff, all of whom had been given their pink slips too.

No one was talking about anything except what all of this meant. We had many more questions than the few answers we had been given. Ellen never really explained how this decision would affect contracts or obligations. We didn't even know whether we were working that day or whether we were all supposed to go home. It turned out that things would pretty much be business as usual until the last day of shooting.

We ended up taping that day, but not according to the schedule. Several hours went by so everyone could absorb what had just happened and attempt to pull ourselves together before getting back to doing what we all loved most. I have no recollection of my particular scenes from the show that day, but boy, I sure do have vivid memories of how this all went down.

Many of the cast hoped another network would pick up the show. After seventy-two years, we thought we had proved our staying power. We had a strong fan base—one of the biggest and best in TV. Why wouldn't someone want this franchise? There were almost immediate rumors all over the Internet that Lifetime was eager to acquire the show, but who knew if anything would materialize? (It didn't.)

What was I going to do?

I tried to tell myself it was no big deal. As actors, we get jobs, we lose jobs. It's all a part of the crazy world of show business.

I tried to tell myself that the world was my oyster. There were a lot of shows that would want me. Right?

I actually asked myself, *What would Susan Lucci do?*

And all I could think was: She'd find something to hawk on the Home Shopping Network!

CHAPTER TWO

My Early Days

Guiding Light had been a pivotal part of my life long before I was cast in the show as Reva. I have vivid memories of being seven years old and coming home from school to find my mom ironing in front of our twenty-inch black-and-white console TV. In the early days of television, people tended to watch the channels that got the strongest reception. In my hometown of Grand Rapids, Michigan, that channel was CBS. So every day of the week my mom watched the entire CBS daytime lineup. She absolutely loved watching her soaps, and *Guiding Light* was the show that was always on the television when I walked through the front door. The show was only fifteen minutes long back then, her tiny daily dose of escapism when she had a chance to disappear from her life and fantasize about the lives of everyone she loved on her show. Even though I never really understood what was going on, my mother was hooked.

After school, I was usually more interested in getting a snack and figuring out how I could beat Mikey, the boy next door, at everything. He was my first crush. He was so cute with his red hair and freckles! But on the days when I couldn't be outside getting into trouble, I'd sit with a slice of warm buttered cinnamon toast in front of the television set and watch *Guiding Light* with my mom. Who would have ever believed that one day my mom would be ironing and watching me on her favorite show?

My husband recently edited all of our home movies and transferred them to DVD. We spent hours watching those old family movies, which brought back so many wonderful memories of my childhood. I smiled as I saw images of my mother and was reminded of the classy dame she was! It didn't matter where they were going; the women of the 1950s and 1960s loved to get dolled up in their dresses, hats, gloves, stilettos, and matching pocketbooks. They were all real lookers, and my mom was no exception!

My dad was and still is the handsomest man I've ever known. He loves to sing, which is where I got my voice and interest in performing. He and my mom were such incredible dancers too. In fact, they met at a dance hall in Dayton, Ohio.

My parents were both great athletes who taught me to play sports at an early age. I was the younger of two girls and a bit of a tomboy, which meant my father treated me like the son he never had. He gave me everything little boys would dream of, including a minibike, baseball bats, footballs, and even a motorcycle. I loved making mud pies, climbing trees, and occasionally getting into schoolyard fights more than playing with my Barbie Dolls, frilly dresses, and girlie things.

I didn't get "girlie" until high school. That was when I became a cheerleader, a member of the homecoming court, and part of Junior Achievement, which was my first introduction to beauty pageants. It was because of that involvement that I was named first runner-up in the Miss Michigan contest. I did a number of pageants as a teenager, which earned me around seven thousand dollars in prize scholarship money I was able to use for college.

I dated quite a bit in high school, but mostly older boys who didn't go to my school. I dealt with a lot of jealousy from girls because I was an overachiever with a ton of extracurricular interests, which meant I wasn't one of the girls who sat around and gossiped with the other girls. I was a guy's girl more than a girl's girl, which oftentimes left me at home alone and in tears, but no one ever knew it. I never wanted anyone else to know that their jealousy could hurt me.

My sister, Karen, was tall, thin, and beautiful, with long legs and the perfect head of thick, straight, naturally blond hair. She was wildly popular with the other girls in school. I was in awe of her ability to have friendships with girls so easily! Karen didn't have to work to be popular. She was instantly liked by everyone. My popularity came through my involvement in outside interests, and from dating guys from other schools.

Was I jealous of her?

You bet!

As kids, my sister and I fought all the time over stupid things that sisters fight about. Mostly she just got aggravated that I always wanted to tag along with her and her boyfriend, Bob, who later became her husband. She married young and moved out of the house when she was nineteen years old. That's when I truly realized how much I loved her and missed her! Today I think of Karen not only as my sister but my closest friend!

I know this isn't in vogue to say, but I was, God help me, a well-adjusted child with good ol' Midwestern values! I was a real hambone who loved being the center of attention. I was definitely a little girl who always had big dreams. When my folks had parties at our house, they usually asked my sister and me to say good night to their guests before we went to bed. I always came up with little skits to perform and made sure they were as long as possible so I could stay up later. Eventually, my dad (though he loved my act) would have to pick me up and carry me to my room or I would have performed all night for the party-goers! My sister was shyer than I was, but always encouraged my little entertaining, albeit dramatic, performances. I think she loved that I usually made a fool of myself!

From the time I was five until I was old enough to want to hang out alone on the beach with my teenage friends, our family went camping every summer. We pitched a tent on the shores of Lake Michigan in Grand Haven. The memories of those week-long camping trips are so vivid in my mind. I can still feel the heat of the sand on the bottoms of my feet and smell the suntan lotion we used back then. Believe it or not, my sister and I used baby oil and Mercurochrome mixed together to give our skin that beautiful deep red burn we craved—and now totally regret!

I spent long summer days jumping waves, bodysurfing with my dad, flirting with the much older lifeguards, building sand castles, and having evening fireside conversations before settling into my sleeping bag for the best sleep ever! I can still smell the charcoal burning in the fire pit where we cooked every meal. I didn't know it then, but I am now certain it was that close fam-ily bonding time that helped give me the confidence and security one needs to survive in the uncertain and cutthroat world of show business. There was something special in my Midwestern upbringing that has kept me grounded over the years. I grew up in a family that was all about commitment and quality time to-gether. Those traits would become essential to helping me create and maintain my own family down the road.

Because of my tomboyish qualities and my desire to be as tough as any kid in the neighborhood, my mom decided to enroll me in dance classes. I think she hoped that maybe I'd get in touch with my more feminine side and develop a little bit of finesse and grace.

I started out taking modern jazz with a wonderful man by the name of Rich Rahn. Rich was also the choreographer for all of the local theater companies in Grand Rapids. There were three community theaters in town at that time: Circle-in-the-Square, the Grand Rapids Civic Theatre, and the Thornapple Players. Rich gave me my start in the performing arts. Through his guidance, I made my theatrical debut in a production of *The Sound of Music* at the age of eleven. I played the part of Louisa von Trapp, the one who put the frogs in the new governesses' beds to scare them off.

Of course that was the role I'd want to play! It was the perfect part for a girl like me.

I especially loved being in that particular production because my mom was working as a seamstress and general chauffeur for the kids in the show. She also appeared as the Blue Fairy in the theater's production of *Pinocchio* and was breathtakingly beautiful!

Once I got the acting bug as a teenager, all I really wanted to do was become a chorus girl.

Yes, a chorus girl.

Why?

Because they always got to wear cool costumes and didn't have to stress out about saying lines.

What could be better than that? I thought.

Oh, did I have a lot to learn.

It wasn't until the summer of my sixteenth year that I woke up and finally figured out there was something better than being the quiet dancer who blends into the background!

My dance teacher convinced me to audition as a dancer for *A Funny Thing Happened on the Way to the Forum*, which was really the beginning of it all for me. The director I auditioned for that day was Don Finn. Oh, my, he was handsome! Tall, with big brown eyes, he wore a sweater thrown over his shoulders like the old Hollywood directors I had seen in the movies. After I danced for him, I was given a script and sheet music to learn the songs from the show, because they wanted me to read for the role of Philia, the young, beautiful heroine. *Oh, boy*, I immediately thought to myself, *that ain't me!*

I prepared the script and worked with the pianist on Philia's song and returned to the stage to finish my audition. When I recited my very first line, people broke out laughing and continued to laugh through my entire audition. (That was good, by the way—it was a musical *comedy*.) When I sang my song, however, they applauded!

That was when it hit me.

I knew what was better than being a chorus girl.

Making people laugh and clap! I wanted to be the next Fanny Brice!

It was at that moment, standing up onstage, that I was officially bitten by the "acting bug."

I got the part and spent the next several weeks preparing for my first opening night. The theater was situated in the middle of the John Ball Park Zoo. In the evening, around the same time the curtain was to go up, it was also feeding time for the animals. Our stage production competed with shrieks, howls, and growls as the animals in the zoo ate their dinner! I'd heard of theater in the park, but this was definitely the first time I ever heard of theater in the zoo! I ended up appearing in about four different shows there over the next two summers.

Due to my immense respect for Don Finn, I applied to and was accepted at Hope College in Holland, Michigan, where Don was a professor of acting and directing. He worked with the wildly talented and funny professor of acting and directing John Tammi, another wonderful teacher. These two men would go on to guide and shape my acting skills and help launch me into the business that would eventually become my career.

Hope College had an excellent summer repertory theater, where I spent two summers working. During my time there, I had the opportunity to play parts in everything from Shakespeare to comedies to musicals. It was the kind of diverse experience every actor should have before going out in the world and attempting to make it big. Rehearsing one show in the morning and afternoon, acting in another show in the evening, striking that show's set the same night, and putting up the set for the next night's show became a regular way of life. It was exhausting and exhilarating all at the same time. The friends I made over those summers at Hope College still remain my dear friends today: Tom Stechschulte, Nancy Sigworth, Alan Suddeth, and Grace Tannehill-Suddeth. Yes, Alan and Grace met at that same theater and, like A.C. and me, got married!

All of these wonderful people were in my wedding party, and I in theirs. In fact, I was Nancy's matron of honor when I was nine months pregnant with my daughter, Rachel. As I started down the aisle, they accidentally started playing "Here Comes the Bride." The mistake got a tremendously loud laugh until the "music man" realized his mistake and stopped before I reached the altar. Luckily, order was restored before the bride made her appearance!

All of us went on to pursue a career doing what we love most—acting and being around the theater. Alan teaches stage combat at workshops all over the country, while his wife, Grace, is a costume designer and assistant at the New York City Opera and New York City Ballet. Tom is an accomplished stage actor and makes his living doing books on tape. He's very good, so look for his name on your next audiobook purchase! And my friend Nancy Sigworth Swann has been the artistic director of a wonderful little theater in Garrison, New York, for many years.

Although the experiences I had at Hope College were unforgettable and invaluable, the best thing that happened to me at Hope was meeting a cute boy named A. C. Weary. A.C. played Bottom in *A Midsummer Night's Dream*. I was Titania, Queen of the Fairies. In the play, Bottom is cursed and turns into a donkey. Titania has been put under a spell as well; when she awakens she falls in love with the first thing she sees . . . which turns out to be the donkey, Bottom!

A.C. had this enormous sculpted jackass head he wore, which he could manipulate from inside his costume with strings to make the eyelashes flutter and the donkey's ears curl. How could you not fall in love with that? It was love at the first bat of those lashes. Yup. I fell hook, line, and sinker for that ass!

Even though I was attracted to him, it took us some time to

finally get together. But once we did, we knew we never wanted to be apart. Like a beautifully scripted scene from any dramatic soap opera, we got together one starlit evening while skinny-dipping in Lake Michigan. He tackled me on a sand dune. We rolled down that dune and that was where it all started. It was romantic, fun, spontaneous, and a long time coming! We began dating, although we both agreed that we could see other people—if we wanted to. After all, we were young and were in college in different states.

The more plays I did at school, the more nervous my dad became that I was going to choose a career that would land me in the poorhouse. He knew how much I loved acting, but also knew how hard it was to make it in show business. His favorite saying all through school was, "Just learn to type, honey. If you can type you'll always have a job." He never said this to be cruel or chauvinistic; he was only giving me advice from his years of experience and from his generation's way of thinking.

It turned out that my dad's words motivated me to work hard enough so I'd never have to type for a living! In my mind, I was born to be an actress, for God's sake! But now, with all of the computers and smartphones, I wish I were a better typist! I guess Dad was right after all.

After two years of my taking every theater course they offered at Hope College, my adviser informed me that I had to start fulfilling my other required courses if I wanted to graduate. I thanked her for the advice and said I wouldn't be finishing my schooling at Hope. By then I had decided to pursue my acting, and I wasn't going to let anything, even college, get in the way.

By the time I made my decision to follow my dream, I had

already scheduled an audition for the American Conservatory Theater in San Francisco. They were holding auditions in Chicago, which was about a six-hour drive from my home in Michigan. My dad agreed to drive me to the audition. I think he was curious to see what this acting thing was all about.

Truth be told, I was still inexperienced when I auditioned for ACT. I was told to prepare two monologues, one classical and one contemporary. For my contemporary monologue I chose to adapt a section from Studs Terkel's *Working*, a collection of interviews about how people feel about their jobs. I picked the prostitute story because I found it more interesting and challenging as a performance piece. It was so far removed from who I was that it was fun to put the mask on and take a chance on this role. Who knew years later I would play a character who would be dubbed "the Slut of Springfield"! Was this a foreshadowing of things to come?

My classical piece was a speech by Queen Margaret from Shakespeare's *Richard III*, another woman who was far removed from who I was. Again, I liked picking roles that allowed me to stretch as an actress and brought me into unexpected territory.

The gentleman conducting the audition was Allen Fletcher, a well-known teacher from ACT. He quite enjoyed my "prostitute," but when I finished my Queen Margaret, he asked me why I chose that speech.

I told him that the monologue spoke to me. I felt so connected to what she was saying in the scene!

"Have you ever read the play?" he asked.

"No," I reluctantly admitted. Alan explained to me that in the play, Queen Margaret is a sixty-year-old woman.

Oh, that.

I *knew* that about the character, but she was just a lot more interesting to me than playing Juliet from *Romeo and Juliet*. I would much rather be a Queen Margaret than a Juliet any day.

I walked out of the audition convinced I'd blown it. I mean, really, who was I to think I could pull off a sixty-year-old queen? I'm just sayin'!

But six weeks later I received the surprise of a lifetime. It was a letter of acceptance from ACT. By the fall of 1976, I was off to San Francisco. When I got the good news, I think my dad was truly excited for my new adventure and for me. My mom, on the other hand, wanted only to send me off with an earthquake kit!

Let me tell you, the program at ACT was *tough*. They made it their job to weed out the weak through exercises in humiliation. It felt more like the military than it did a conservatory, because they tore us down before building us back up. The acting exercises were designed to help actors get in touch with their deepest emotions by exposing their most personal secrets that could be manipulated into a "character's" psyche. Some actors were unable to recover from the emotional exposure and ended up quitting the program as a result of the raw display, which oftentimes made you feel naked and vulnerable.

As much as I wanted to dig deep, I really didn't have dramatic wounds to open. The only wounds I had from childhood were really normal things, like adolescent jealousies about someone's boyfriend or my dad calling me out whenever I'd open the freezer door for ice cream. Other people in my class had real traumas that they were dealing with, I guess, which gave them someplace to go emotionally or a frame of reference that I simply didn't have. There is a method of acting that some actors rely on called substitution. That is when you use real-life images and memories as substitutes for situations that may arise in a scene. For example, if a character's son is in a car accident and is being rushed into surgery, some actors would substitute someone from their real life, be it a child, sibling, spouse, parent, or good friend, to help them imagine how they should react. That method was a distraction to me. If I tried it I would get so completely lost thinking about my own loved one in that situation that I'd forget it was just pretend. It's not real; it's acting, right?

Whatever! There were plenty of times I had to remind myself of that, and still it was often very emotional.

One of the most important things I learned at the conservatory was that no one could *learn* to act. Acting is inherent; it's in your blood and in your bones. You can learn to sharpen your skills or get better, but the plain and simple truth is that you either have the talent or you don't. Only the strong survived at ACT, and they were the individuals invited back to face another year at the conservatory. Although I was invited to return the following year, I graciously declined and left the program after only one year. To be totally candid, I thought their approach was bullshit. I gained more knowledge and experience by exploring the underworld of San Francisco in the 1970s than exploring my own psyche and all that theater-training baloney! I learned significantly more about acting in my two years in the theater department at Hope College than I did at ACT. And my years in Junior Achievement taught me at an early age that learning by doing was the only way to go!

After my year at ACT, I felt I was ready to find out what the world had to offer. I believed I had the tools needed to apply myself to any role. My feeling has always been that if you trust the writing, trust your acting partner, and honestly believe in the life you're portraying, you'll be successful at making your audience believe it too. That philosophy has never failed me yet.

After leaving San Francisco, I moved to Chicago to begin the rest of my life! Typically, a lot of actors head to New York or Los Angeles, but I felt the need to be closer to my family. Moving back to Michigan wasn't an option unless I wanted to end up in a typing pool after all, so I settled down in the Windy City to see if I could make a go of things. Luckily, Chicago ended up being the right move for me. I had heard there were a lot of good-money jobs in Chicago, plus I wanted to do musical comedy and thought there might be some chance to work with the great Steppenwolf Theatre Company.

I moved in with my friend Nancy Sigworth, whom I knew from Hope College. We lived in the heart of Old Town, Chicago. By this time, A.C. was living with me on and off—mostly off, because he had a thriving career in regional theater all over the country, which meant he spent a lot of time on the road. Somehow, that openness and lack of neediness worked for our relationship. We were both passionately pursuing our careers, supporting each other in that endeavor in any way we could.

Shortly after I settled in, I landed my first real agent, Vic Perillo, whom I affectionately called "the bear" because he looked like a cuddly little bear. He stood about five and a half feet tall, with a headful of bushy black hair.

Because of Vic's incredibly hard work and my determination, I was able to work in many areas of the business, including commercials, which got me my coveted AFTRA and SAG union cards. I also did live industrial shows, which allowed me to perform at big conventions all over the country. The shows were written like mini Broadway musicals, with the "star" being whatever product they were pushing. I danced and sang my little heart out over Whirlpool washers and dryers, Kohler tubs and toilets, and Standard Oil. These tours were tiring, but they paid very well back in the 1970s.

I sometimes worked with Nancy Grahn, another fantastic actress and friend, who went on to become a popular soap diva known as Alexis on *General Hospital*. Back in the day, we both had Vic as our agent in Chicago. He also represented the handsome Steve Fletcher, who went on to work at *One Life to Live*.

Vic had an eye for actors he knew would excel in daytime. He frequently took his clients on junkets to New York and Los Angeles, where we had the opportunity to audition for the casting directors of most of the soaps being shot on both coasts. On one of the audition tours, I met a woman named Betty Rea, the casting director for *Guiding Light*. She gave me a bit part for a single day of work, as a receptionist for a character named Roger Thorpe! At the time, I had no idea who his character was or the power of the actor playing him, Michael Zaslow. I barely had three lines in the scene, which I was lucky to spit out, because I was so enamored with the man they called "Zaz." I thought we had an incredible chemistry together and desperately hoped that my receptionist part would turn into a contract role on *Guiding Light*. (A girl can dream, can't she?) I am not exactly sure why Betty cast me, but I believe she did it as a favor to Vic. She obviously admired his drive and determination in bringing young actors to New York just to get the experience of auditioning. If they were lucky enough to get a part, even a bit part like mine, it would have all been worth it.

I truly believe that if I'd never met Vic Perillo I would never have even thought of spending the next thirty years playing four dynamic characters on various soaps. I want to thank Mr. Perillo for helping guide my career on this path, because he opened my eyes to the possibilities in daytime when I might have otherwise overlooked its potential.

I was so fortunate to have had the wealth of theatrical experience I already had by the time I moved to Chicago. I worked a lot in the Drury Lane circuit, the theater circuit in and around Chicago composed of four theaters that are mostly in large hotels around the city. The shows were top-notch, drawing well-known performers from all over the country. I acted with the legendary Ricardo Montalban in the play *Accent on Youth*. If you look in the dictionary under *gentleman*, there would be a picture of Ricardo! He was the epitome of elegance and class. When my mother and sister came to see the show, Ricardo was so kind, treating them as if they were his own family. He always insisted on taking all of the women out after the show, when he ordered for all of us and always paid the bill. He was old-school in every way. He held open doors, pulled out my chair, helped me with my coat, and always made me feel special.

In 1977, I also worked with James Farentino and Michele Lee in Odets's downbeat drama about a suicidal actor, *The Big Knife*. James and Michele were married at the time . . . barely. One suggestion to all of you budding actors out there: Never work with a couple on the brink of divorce. It's scary! They'd have an argument and he'd take it out on me every night on-stage! The audience got a dream performance filled with intensity and strength, but for me, it felt like borderline abuse.

I also worked with the amazing Nehemiah Persoff in that same production. Nehemiah was a consummate professional whom I absolutely adored. Like Ricardo, he was old Hollywood, an actor's actor who loved what he did. He was generous in wanting to share his knowledge and experience with young actors such as myself. The legendary talent I had the privilege of working alongside during those years was nothing short of fantastic. It was truly the stuff that acting dreams are made of.

By 1978, I was in the Chicago company of *Godspell* at the Drury Lane Water Tower when my agent called to tell me that I'd been offered a three-day role on *One Life to Live*. We'd seen the casting director, Mary Jo Slater, during our previous trip to New York, and she wanted me for the part. It was a great opportunity, but I didn't know if I could take the job because of my commitment to *Godspell*. Fortunately, when I went to the producers of the play with my dilemma, they said, "Go. Come back when you're done." Gracious, to say the least, and very much appreciated.

In the end, I never returned to *Godspell*. Miraculously, three days turned into three months of episodes playing Bonnie Harmer, a Patty Hearst type of misunderstood terrorist! I knew there wasn't going to be a future for this particular character, because she was there to kill people. Killers don't often have longevity on soaps, so I used the experience for what it was—a short-term job that actually paid and offered some practical exposure in a field I hadn't even considered. I actually thought I'd return to Chicago to do more theater.

Coincidentally, A.C., who was then living in New York, had been cast in the same show playing a psychopathic stalker named Dick Grant. What a pair we were! We had a load of fun working together for those few weeks. When each day was finished, we painted the town, exploring theater and other arts around New York City. A.C. was actually doing double duty starring in *The Tooth of Crime*, a Sam Shepard play about an old rock and roller doing battle with a younger rival. I often went to see A.C. in the show and would fall in love with him all over again as he strutted across the stage in tight black leather pants!

Although I wasn't specifically thinking I would end up acting on a soap, my stint on *One Life to Live* was all I needed to make the decision to officially move to New York. Up to this point, my relationship with A.C. had been on and off because we were living in two different cities and both of us were busy, but we still maintained our deep love for each other. After spending this time together, I knew I wanted to spend the rest of my life with him. It was time to take our relationship and my career to the next level. To do that, I would have to pull the trigger to leave Chicago and make the move to the Big Apple.

CHAPTER THREE

New York, New York

We rented our first apartment in New York City in 1979. It was a wonderful little one-bedroom, third-floor walk-up apartment in a brownstone on Seventy-fifth Street between Central Park West and Columbus Avenue. The Upper West Side of Manhattan was such a great neighborhood. It still is, but in those days, people would still sit on their front stoops and greet you with a pleasant "Good morning" when you walked by. The rent was a bit expensive for us, four hundred and fifty dollars a month, but we somehow managed to scrape the money together.

A.C. was working the theater scene a lot and always managed to land a national commercial when we needed it most! That's how our life together has always been. If I wasn't working, he was, and vice versa. We furnished our apartment with discarded things we found on the street. You'd be amazed by what other people throw away! You know the old saying "One man's trash is another man's treasure"? Well, we were young and considered those street finds our treasures. We furnished our apartment with an eclectic mix of paintings, stained glass that A.C. made, lots of antiques, and a glass table with a baby bottle attached to it so our pet rabbit could drink water from it! We had the only paper-trained rabbit in the neighborhood!

My relationship with A.C. had been progressing nicely for

the past three years, although it wasn't the most conventional of romances. Although he was based in New York, he started working on a nighttime series in California, so he would fly out to the West Coast every few weeks or so. Whenever A.C. was in town, we'd hit the streets, shuffling through other people's dreck. I loved the results. We collected everything from headboards and bookshelves to a table and chairs that would otherwise have been lost forever. A.C. refinished or refurbished the items, often making them look better than new.

A very smart person once told me, "It is where you go home to at the end of the day that is the most important thing in our business." No matter how big or small your "home" may be, it has to be a place that feels safe and secure. It has to be a place where you can decompress and feel at peace at the end of a day of disappointment and rejection. That was how I felt in our home. It helped that I had my honey's loving arms to cuddle in too!

A.C. and I had joked about getting married any number of times, but one of us always managed to change the subject. If memory serves me correctly, in the summer of 1980, we were in our teeny-tiny kitchen making dinner when we started talking about having a baby. I believe I said I'd love to have a kid but I wanted to be married first. Hint, hint, wink, wink!

A.C. said something like "Are you asking me to marry you?"

I said, "If you want me to have your babies, then yes, I'm asking you to marry me!" And that was when he very sweetly, through tears and giggles, asked me to be his wife.

We got married in August of 1981 in the presence of two hundred friends and family from all walks of our life together.

Our bridal party consisted of our closest friends who were in that same summer theater group where we met, along with my sister, his brother, and two of his sisters as well.

We got married in a church in my hometown of Grand Rapids, Michigan. Our minister, the good Reverend Gaylord, was a wonderfully gentle man whom I'd known for many years through his son, who attended the same elementary and high school I did. Since A.C. and I are both actors, I think the reverend was a bit nervous that someone was going to interrupt the service and start something as a gag! So he raced through the ceremony. In his haste, he totally forgot to say, "You may now kiss the bride!" For years I didn't know whether we were officially married because we hadn't sealed the deal with a kiss!

The wedding was a blast, and included skinny-dipping by many of our guests in the hotel pool! But one of my favorite memories is from the rehearsal dinner, when A.C.'s brother, Ralph (who was twenty years old at the time), got up and made a toast none of us would ever forget.

"My brother finally had the nerve to ask Kim to marry him! It's a good thing he did, because if he didn't, I was going to!"

It got thunderous laughter from all, but I had a feeling he meant it! I love that kid!

After my "terrorist" on *One Life to Live* died in a hail of bullets (or was I carted off to jail after turning myself in to the Llanview Police Department and confessing all I had done? I can't remember!), I found myself unemployed. The time had come for me to do what every actor in New York does at one time or another: start pounding the pavement. Day after day, I spent my time going to open calls I found in *Backstage* magazine. *Backstage* listed all of the available auditions for the week, so it was like the bible for actors looking for their next job. As long as you were a member of the Actors' Equity union, you could go to any of these open "cattle call" auditions. If you had an agent, you would be assigned a specific time; if you didn't, you were assigned a number and waited—sometimes all day—to be seen. What a trip! One of my most memorable auditions was for a production of *King Lear* that the great director Elia Kazan was producing, with Richard Burton playing the part of Lear. I really went on this call only so I could get more experience auditioning in New York. I never expected to be standing onstage in front of Mr. Kazan in an empty Broadway theater reading for the role of Lear's youngest daughter, Cordelia. Mr. Kazan actually directed my audition, which I can only describe as a true thrill and honor for a young up-and-comer. With his help, I felt confident that the role was mine! And I think it would have been, except, for whatever reason, the project was never produced. It was, as they say in the industry, "shelved for future consideration."

Another audition that will forever be emblazoned in my memory was for the musical *Funny Face*, starring Sandy Duncan and directed and choreographed by the wunderkind Tommy Tune. Nancy, my friend and former roommate from Chicago, who was now living in New York as well, went with me to the open call for singers who could dance or dancers who could sing. I fashioned myself a "triple threat": an *actress* who could not only sing but move really well. I mean, I'm not a classically trained dancer, but I can move.

The first order of business was to sing eight bars of any song.

If you got past that portion of the audition, you were asked to wait for the dancing portion. Nancy and I both made it over the first hurdle with relative ease and were off to the holding area for the dancers. The hallway was filled to capacity with tall, beautiful, leggy dancers. Suddenly we were surrounded by real chorus girls. I don't know what I was thinking when I dreamed of being a chorus girl. I mean, c'mon! They had legs that didn't end and bodies that rocked. Still, Nancy and I looked at each other and thought, *What the hell!*

Unfortunately, the producers expected us to be accomplished *tap dancers* too. This was not part of my repertoire! But I did the best I could. I put on a pair of tap shoes and said, "Feet, don't fail me now!" I was so nervous when it came time to go out on the stage, my toes actually curled up inside my tap shoes, which made it impossible for any sound to emanate from my taps. I also succeeded in getting in the way of all the other very accomplished tappers. It was worse than an episode of *I Love Lucy*! You know the shows where Lucy takes the stage and messes up Ricky's performance? Yeah, it was that bad!

After an excruciating two minutes, I was thankful to be asked to leave by none other than Tommy Tune himself. Hey, at least he noticed me! He probably won't remember this audition, but it's one that I've never forgotten!

The whole "cattle call" audition routine was interesting and fun for about a month, but it wasn't getting me any work. The only way to make that happen was for me to get an agent in New York. A.C. was already signed with the J. Michael Bloom Agency, so he was able to set up an appointment for me to meet with the agents there before I looked elsewhere. It helped that I already had quite an extensive résumé from Chicago. Fortunately, before I could say, "Get me a job!" I was signed. Michael Bloom was just what you'd expect: an agent straight out of central casting. He was a wonderfully flamboyant man, generous, bawdy, a fantastic host who wasn't afraid to chase you around his office if he found you attractive. Not me, mind you, but boy, did he love A.C.! It didn't matter to Michael that A.C. was *my* man! Michael teased me mercilessly about how he was going to convert A.C. to being gay and steal him away.

Michael was a good man and a wonderful agent. As his agency became more recognized, his client list expanded and he had to hire a number of new agents. One of those agents was Brian Reardon, who became one of the most important influences in shaping my career. Brian was a straight shooter when it came to negotiating contracts. He never forced me to take a job I didn't want. He always sat and listened as I tried to flesh out the pros and cons of any job. I adored the man.

Now that I had a new agent locked up, it was time to let the games begin! I continued to audition for musicals and plays, but having an agent made everything much easier. All I had to do was show up at the given address to audition, do my thing, and let my agents handle the rest!

Over time, I came close to landing a number of Broadway and off-Broadway shows, but for some reason, it simply wasn't happening. I'd get callback after callback, but then never got the part. I felt like the perpetual bridesmaid! Maybe it simply wasn't meant to be. And then, in the fall of 1979, Brian got a call for me to audition for a soap opera called *The Doctors*. The producers were casting a replacement for an actress named Kathleen

Turner, who had decided that she wanted to try other things. Kathleen had herself replaced Kathryn Harrold. It appeared that I had some pretty big shoes to fill.

At the time, I didn't know anything about the show. I'd never seen it; nor was I familiar with any of the actors. I read the breakdown for the role and agreed to go on the audition.

I must say, I felt very comfortable in the character's shoes. Sometimes as an actor, you just know when it's right.

I mean, *really?*

Who would be better to play the role of Nola Dancy Aldrich, the troublemaking, gold-digging daughter of a salt-of-the-earth father who owned the town's pub?

I ended up nailing my audition. So when Brian called to tell me that they'd offered me the role, I was thrilled but I wasn't surprised. I felt I was born to play the part, but I had to make it clear that I wouldn't play the character the way Kathleen did. She did a great job—she made a great bitch—but I felt the character needed other colors. I always try to find the vulnerable side to the characters I play. Initially, Nola was written to be a hard-hearted bitch, and that is the way Kathleen played her. She was an obvious gold digger who cared only about marrying into money. When I took over, the writers were willing to take the character a little deeper by delving into why she was so hard and money-obsessed. The writers created story lines that showed her relationship with her family and why she fought so hard for so many years to achieve a certain lifestyle. When Nola finally figured out that her life was complicated because of where she came from, it allowed me to play her in a more vulnerable way.

I think the writers decided to make Nola more sympathetic

when they realized that I could cry on cue. Honest to God, they know audiences love to see people cry on the tube! As I always say, "Give 'em what they want!"

The Doctors was taped at the NBC studios in Rockefeller Center, which in itself was a thrill. There was always so much going on in that building. *Saturday Night Live* was just taking off, and it was common to run into John Belushi, Dan Aykroyd and Gilda Radner. Whenever I'd see one of them, I'd get so star-struck I could never say a word.

The local news was also shot in that building, as was *The Phil Donahue Show.* Being in that part of the city, especially during the holidays, was exciting. I was proud to tell people I worked at Rockefeller Center. Weather permitting, I left my apartment on West Seventy-fifth Street at six fifteen each morning, laced my feet into my roller skates, and skated through the most beautiful park in the world, Central Park, as the sun came up over the horizon. At that time of the morning, with no one around but the taxis and a few joggers, New York is so peaceful it can be described only as magical.

Upon my arrival at Rockefeller Center, the game was on! The floors were the smoothest, fastest surface you could find in the city for polyurethane wheels! Of course, skating through the building was strictly forbidden, but I never had to worry about the guards until I'd reach the elevators, which meant I had about three hundred yards to play on every morning.

Our shooting day began at seven o'clock in the morning, and we typically wrapped no later than two in the afternoon; we had to wrap then because the local news began at three o'clock and needed to use our equipment. After work, the cast and crew finished our day downstairs at the corner bar, Hurley's, where most of us could be found by four. We'd have a libation and happy-hour munchies and discuss the silliness of our jobs for the next two hours. It was an ideal way to unwind after being on the set all day. When I was finished, I'd strap on my skates and head back through the park and home to the arms of my sweetie!

I had my first kiss on television with the gorgeous actor Glenn Corbett, who played Jason Aldrich. Jason was the eldest son of the richest family in town, and Jason's mother, Mona, hated that her son was smitten with this little guttersnipe. Nola and Jason already had a real love-hate relationship going when I took over the role, so although it wasn't *their* first kiss, it was mine.

I remember it like it happened yesterday. Glenn was about fifteen years my senior, but oh, my! He was tall and manly, with dazzling blue eyes and dark hair. I had no idea what to expect from my first on-screen kiss. Thank God it wasn't a bed scene as well, because I would have been a complete mess of nerves.

When the cameras rolled and Glenn took me in his arms and planted one on me . . . va-va-voom! I was smitten! He was so gentle and sweet. He also knew I was a nervous wreck. He incessantly teased me about it for months afterward.

That first kiss led to countless others, all memorable in their own way. Nola was primarily involved with Jason throughout the years I was on the show, and I got very comfortable kissing Glenn. But toward the end of my four years on *The Doctors*, I got to play love scenes with a dashing twenty-one-year-old actor who was new to the show, by the name of Alec Baldwin. This was his first professional acting job, and he was a natural.

I was sitting in the green room with several other actresses on the show when Alec tested for the role of Billy Aldrich. It was "that voice" that had all of us running to the control room *begging* the bosses to hire him. Luckily they did, and Alec and I became fast friends.

In the meantime, and much to my delight, A.C. and I became pregnant for the first time. Unfortunately, the show didn't share my bliss, as my weight ballooned some fifty pounds within the first several months. I was huge, and it didn't help that I was eating a pint of Häagen-Dazs ice cream every night. The store was right on our block, so I had easy access to whatever my craving of the day was—usually Vanilla Swiss Almond and Maple Walnut. The producers were nervous, but worked with me to disguise my growing belly. The harsh truth was that there was soon no hiding my pregnancy behind hats or sets, so they wrote it into the show, having Nola get pregnant along with me!

Being pregnant as an actress has its share of challenges, but maybe the worst is how self-conscious you can become. I had seen it happen to other actresses on the show, as the director grew frustrated trying to get the shot he wanted without catching her belly on camera. It was very lucky for me when Nola became pregnant so I didn't have to worry about that.

Working with Alec Baldwin was always a ball. He is so naturally funny. Everything you see of him on *30 Rock* comes from his intelligent humor. He's also incredibly knowledgeable about everything from classical music to law to politics. While it might have been a little intimidating at first, Alec never judged anyone for their opinions or lack of knowledge. After I became pregnant, it was Alec who took over the husbandly duties for A.C.

when I was at the studio. If I craved egg-salad sandwiches with dill pickles on white Wonder bread, Alec would take off for the NBC commissary and return with egg salad in hand! He is a smart man who instinctively knew he didn't want to deal with a pregnant mama bear when she was hungry. Alec was always sure to stay one step ahead. We forged a friendship back then that I cherish to this very day. Alec still makes it a point to come out to our house in Montclair for our New Year's Eve parties whenever he's in town. He will hop in a limo and be there to play a round or two of charades, stay for a couple of hours until midnight, and head to his next party. I am so grateful for his friendship, love, and support. Except he still hasn't asked me to be a guest star on that little show of his, *30 Rock*! What's that about, Alec?

The powers that be were so nervous that I'd go into labor at the studio that they wrote a part for A.C. to play on the show so he'd be close by—just in case. A.C. played Thor, a worldly sailor with whom it was revealed Nola had secretly had an affair while engaged to Billy. Nola had convinced Billy the baby was his, thinking she would never see Thor again. Lo and behold, he showed up in town to claim his woman and unborn child so they could sail away into the sunset together (I had decided to leave the show after the baby was born).

I'll never forget A.C. having to play his very first bed scene on television with me while I was nine months pregnant with his real-life child. Doing those scenes crossed a line for us. By this time I had done many love scenes on the show, so I was used to the impersonal nature of it all, but this was A.C.'s first, and it was doubly challenging that it was me. You might think it would be easier to film a love scene with someone you actually love, but in fact the reverse is true. It's like giving away your intimate and personal self. Basically, when you're doing a love scene with your real-life partner, it feels like you're making a sex tape and the entire crew is peeking in on your private life in the bedroom! We giggled all the way through those scenes, with Alec standing off camera busting a gut as well. Ah, the romance of it all!

Working on a soap is a great training ground to learn how to think on your feet. Sometimes things happen on a set and you've got to be able to roll with the moment or risk having to start the scene all over again. In the late 1970s and well into the 1980s, most sets used cue cards—cards with all the lines, held up by real human beings. The cue card holders stood just off the set, so anytime you forgot a line you could glance at the card and see your next bit of dialogue.

That was the theory, anyway. The guys who held the cards were well-meaning union guys who, God bless them, were bored stiff with their jobs. Every time I needed a line the guys were usually a card or two behind. I found it nearly impossible to use the damn things. So instead, I decided to start learning everyone's lines so I would never, ever be lost in a scene.

Mistakes by the actors were very costly in those early days. If an actor had to stop because he couldn't remember a line or didn't hit his mark, the producers were very unhappy; it meant they would have to go into an edit bay to fix the error, which was expensive and very time-consuming. They had to literally cut and paste the tape together where they'd made the edit. They would tell us all the time that it cost about fifteen hundred dollars every time one of us screwed up!

Yikes!

Being the new kid on the block, I didn't want to be the one to cost the show that much money.

I didn't want anyone else to mess up either. I was always looking out for my fellow actors. If someone else blanked, I'd just say his lines for him so we wouldn't have to stop rolling. I remember one scene with Jim Pritchett, who played Dr. Matt Powers. I could tell he had forgotten his line, so in character I said, "I'm sure if I were you, I'd want to tell me that . . ." and then said his line for him!

When the scene was over, Jim knew something weird had happened but didn't realize that I had just said both my lines and his. When I watched the show on air, it was obvious that something went terribly wrong, but hey, I still saved the show fifteen hundred dollars for the edit.

There have been times over the years when I found it necessary to change some of my dialogue, but I always tried to make those adjustments during our rehearsals so I didn't confuse the other actors when it came time to shoot the scene. Sometimes I'd insist on changing the dialogue because I didn't feel it was right for the character or that it was something she would say, and other times, if the writer or director was able to somehow convince me to keep the dialogue, I would back down. We always discussed what we should do before any changes were made.

This was even more important back when soaps aired live instead of on tape. I recall hearing a story many years ago about an actor who went off script on *The Doctors* during a live show. Allegedly, the actor was doing a scene on an airplane and opened the wrong door. He was supposed to open the door to the bathroom. Instead, he opened the door to the plane—while it was "in the air." While the character wasn't slated to die that day, the director was forced to kill him with that fall out of the airplane. Back in those days of live television, there weren't a lot of options but to roll with whatever happened. Poor guy never even saw it coming!

The years I spent on *The Doctors* were so valuable to me. I learned discipline, and how to be prepared, how to learn lines and to protect my character. The show itself was always on the chopping block for almost the whole time I was there. We never knew if the next thirteen-week extension would be our last. That uncertainty went on for all four years I played Nola. The show never really garnered the ratings that it had in its heyday and eventually went off the air in 1982, three months after I left. Still, I milked all the joy I could out of it while I was there.

My time on *The Doctors* not only allowed me to get my feet wet, but also allowed me to learn from some of the best actors in daytime at the time, including Jada Rowland, James Pritchett, Lydia Bruce, the gorgeous Meg Mundy, and one of the funniest men I've ever known, David O'Brien.

But I believe I learned the most during that time from an actress who to this day still mesmerizes me, Elizabeth Hubbard. I can remember doing these big party scenes that everyone hated because they were long and boring days. But I'd watch Liz Hubbard in those scenes and become intrigued by the life she'd created for herself to stay in a scene in which she didn't even have any dialogue. One day, I asked her how she maintained focus in a scene where she never spoke.

"Oh, darling, I just try to figure out who *farted*," Liz casually answered.

After she told me that, I made sure to watch the air shows on party days. Sure enough, that was exactly what she did. I used her trick many times over the years. It certainly kept me "in the scene" with a twinkle in my eye!

I ended up playing Nola well into my ninth month of pregnancy so we could tie up her story before I left. It was important to make sure there were no loose ends, because there was no chance I'd be coming back. I was eager and excited to be at home with the baby for as long as she needed me. I was elated and overjoyed to become a mother. I wanted to savor every moment.

I finally got the chance to thank Kathleen Turner in person for leaving her role on *The Doctors*. In 1980, I played a look-alike who switches identities with Kathleen's character in a film called *Body Heat*.

That was bizarre!

I'd replaced her on *The Doctors* and now here I was playing her look-alike. Don't get me wrong. I admire Kathleen Turner, but it felt a little bit like I was stalking her!

Body Heat was the first major film for a few of us in that cast, including Mickey Rourke, Ted Danson, Kathleen, and me. It was William Hurt's second big role. We all had a great time on the shoot, even though we were filming in West Palm Beach, Florida, in one-hundred-degree temperatures and ninety percent humidity. The title *Body Heat* was not a fabrication!

It was hot! And I am not just talking about the weather. The movie was pretty darn steamy too!

I was able to spend a little bit of time with Richard Crenna while I was on location and came to admire him so much. He was such a gentleman and gave me some great insights on shooting films. He told me to always remember to "save it for the close-up"! I had a tendency to give and give on every take to the point where, when it was time to shoot my close-up, I was spent! He assured me that it wasn't being selfish to save something. It was called preservation. I had a small but pivotal role in the film. I remember the director, Lawrence Kasdan, told me that the scene when I was to turn around in the gazebo after William Hurt says, "Hey, lady, ya wanna fuck?" was going to be an extreme close-up on me. He said my face would fill the entire screen at movie houses all over the world—so make it good!

No pressure there!

I was pleased with the end result and I guess moviegoers enjoyed it too. I had more people recognize me from those thirty seconds in that film than my four years on *The Doctors*!

CHAPTER FOUR

The Role of Mom Will Be Played by Kim Zimmer

My greatest role, as "Mom," was cast June 20, 1982, the day our daughter, Rachel, was born. Like most first-time mothers, I went into labor and raced to the hospital too early. They shaved me, gave me an enema, and then just monitored my every move for hours. I probably should have gone home, but it was my first baby, so I was too nervous to leave the hospital once I was there. I spent twenty-two hours in labor before Rachel made her grand entrance into the world. The staff at New York's Roosevelt Hospital was wonderful. I think a few of the nurses may have recognized me, which was good and bad. When word spread that I was there, every nurse who hadn't yet met me came by to say hello. Normally, I never mind meeting fans—but when you're in labor with contractions less than two minutes apart, well, let's just say I wasn't my most gracious! I am certain I scared a few of those poor gals right out of the room.

A.C. and I were the first among our friends to have a kid. Our friends gave Rachel the nickname "Danger Baby," because she was so easy and well behaved, she made everyone else want to have a baby. They said there would be a world full of babies if every baby was like Rachel.

We were those parents who took the baby everywhere we went. We forced her on all of our friends, took her to the movies and out to restaurants. We made the baby adapt to our lifestyle, which I highly recommend to all new parents. We had a little canvas carrier we hauled her around in and a portable Sassy Seat we could attach to any table. If we went to parties, Rachel usually came along. She'd cruise around until she got tired. When she pooped out, we'd lay her down on the pile of coats that were on the bed, where she cuddled up until she fell asleep.

In late 1982, our family decided to relocate to Los Angeles so A.C. could pursue some acting opportunities on the West Coast. Fortunately, A.C. did well in L.A. and got work on numerous pilots and series. As for me, I was enjoying being a mom and living on the beach in Venice. I was content with how everything was going in my life and in no hurry to settle into another job. At least, that was what I kept telling myself, until my agent in New York called to tell me the producers of *One Life to Live* wanted to offer me a three-year contract.

I was surprised and delighted to be asked back. This time I'd be playing a mysterious character named Contessa Echo DiSavoy. I wanted to go to New York to pursue this role, while A.C. wanted to stay in Los Angeles, where he was working steadily. Long distance had always been a part of our relationship, so I didn't think it would have a negative impact to spend some time living on opposite coasts. I figured I would take Rachel back to New York with me so A.C. could continue to pursue his career in California. We were the type of couple who supported each other's dreams, even if it meant we'd be apart from time to time.

After discussing the pros and cons, we both agreed that the offer to return to *One Life to Live* was nearly impossible to refuse. So Rachel and I packed our bags and moved back to New

York City so I could begin work on the show. We figured we would just travel back and forth to see each other every other weekend.

Right!

Although it sounded promising in theory, it never happened. After three months of trying to make things work, A.C. decided to move back to New York so we could be together as a family. A.C. said he needed to be with Rachel and me more than he needed to be in Los Angeles. So he put his career on hold and moved back to New York to become a Mr. Mom—a huge sacrifice and the most romantic gesture.

A.C. made our first house a home and was basically a stay-at-home dad. Although he would slip away to do a play here and there, he made the choice to be with Rachel, something I will always love and appreciate about my husband. His choice to be with our children those years made my career possible. He is the most selfless and supportive husband any gal could dream of having. I am one lucky woman to have a guy like him.

A.C. was getting to spend quality time with Rachel, and I was having a blast playing the wacky Echo DiSavoy, who came to Llanview to destroy Clint Buchanan's life. It was a privilege to work with Clint Ritchie, the original Clint Buchanan. Clint played a cowboy on *One Life to Live* and was a cowboy in real life too. He had a ranch in northern California, where he spent most of his time off from the show. He was a New York City cowboy who was out of place in Manhattan, but who was a great man's man. He loved to party hard, didn't suffer fools, and always told it like it was. I loved working with him so much.

The first time Echo tried to seduce Clint was in a swimming

pool. I had to wear a bathing suit and he was in swim trunks—which was oddly uncomfortable for me. The scene was shot at the YMCA in New York City. Echo was out to break up Clint's marriage to Vicki, played by the wonderful Erika Slezak. Echo's partner in crime was Dorian Lord, played by the unbelievably talented Robin Strasser. Dorian was archrivals with Vicki, so she had motivation to encourage the affair.

As much fun as the character was to play, being back at *One Life to Live* wasn't all smooth sailing, and it didn't last as long as I had hoped. One day, I walked up to the office to get my holds for the next two weeks. Holds are the dates you receive about a week in advance that let you know when you're expected to work. The production secretary gave me a weird look when I asked about my holds.

"Uh, I believe next week is your last week of holds," she said.

"What?" I asked. "That can't be. I'm signed to a three-year contract!" But of course I knew that, every thirteen weeks, the show had the option to let me out of my contract. And today was the end of my first thirteen-week cycle.

Well, the secretary didn't know what to tell me about the situation, so I asked to speak to the executive producer, Jean Arley.

"She's actually at lunch right now," she said.

Great, I thought. *Jean is out enjoying a broccoli soufflé while I'm standing in the office dying.*

I decided not to put a call in to my agent, because I was sure it had to be some kind of huge misunderstanding. I believed everything was going to be resolved as soon as I could speak to Jean.

It wasn't easy, but I forced myself to go about my business. But as time passed and the lunch hour began nearing the dinner hour, I knew there was indeed a real problem. I couldn't shake that feeling you get when you know you're about to get bad news. I spent the entire afternoon walking around on pins and needles.

When Jean finally came to find me, the look of doom in her eyes confirmed my worst fears. They wouldn't be picking up my option on my next thirteen-week cycle. She explained that my character, though wildly popular, was no longer needed. Jean gave me this devastating news during a five-minute crew break and then expected me to go right back to work!

The message was loud and clear: *Don't let the door hit you on the ass on your way out!*

After I was let go, I heard rumors that my popularity had ruffled the feathers of one of the leading actresses on the show who was dating one of the executives at ABC, and she pulled some strings. As the old saying goes, "It's not who you know; it's who you blow!"

Boom.

I was *gone.*

To say I panicked would be an understatement. I had just relocated my family all the way to New York City, only to have my secure three-year job disappear after three months. Let's just say it's a good thing I believe everything happens for a reason, because I was so devastated that I could have easily lost my drive to keep acting after being let go from *One Life to Live.*

I went on numerous auditions right away. I was desperate to find a job. I read for anything and everything. My last episodes of *One Life to Live* were just airing when my agent called to say he had an audition for me on *Guiding Light*.

Guiding Light was created by Irna Phillips and began as a fifteen-minute daily NBC Radio serial on January 25, 1937 (luckily, the birth date of *Guiding Light* and not my own!). The show was actually canceled twice during its years on radio. When Procter & Gamble canceled the show in 1941, they received seventy-five thousand protest letters demanding it be put back on the air. General Mills picked up the rights and resurrected the radio program, until it too canceled the show in 1946.

CBS Radio moved the show from Chicago to Hollywood so they could have access to more talent, and by June 1947, once again, *Guiding Light* was back on the radio. By 1949, it made one last move to air live from New York City, where most soap operas originated, especially in the 1950s, 1960s, and 1970s. The show made its debut on CBS television on June 30, 1952.

I felt so burned by my last experience working in daytime that at first I told my agent flat out that I was dead set against working on another soap opera. He insisted that I reconsider and at least take a look at the character breakdown before making any final decision. He also informed me that the casting director had specifically requested me to come in to read.

This was Betty Rea, who I believe is the best casting director in the business, and is the same woman who had given me my bit part a few years earlier. Betty oozed class, style, and grace out of every pore. She also had an amazing sense of humor! She was famous for being able to transform herself into whatever character necessary so she could help with the read. When you auditioned with Betty, she gave you one hundred percent support to help you get the role. It wasn't something she did just for me—no, Betty did this for everyone, because the bottom line was that she simply loved actors.

My first meeting was with Betty so she could explain the character of Reva Shayne to me: She was from Tulsa, Oklahoma. Her father was a wildcatter and her mama cleaned the Lewis mansion, taking her little girl along to play while she worked. Reva lived her childhood in the shadow of the Lewises and swore she'd be one of them someday.

Reva fought with the Lewis boys like they were siblings, but she fell in love with young Joshua. When he left town, she married his brother Billy but they divorced, and now she was coming to Springfield to break up Billy's romance with Vanessa Chamberlain. She was being paid by Alan Spaulding, who was hoping that Vanessa would leave Billy and fall into his arms. Reva was an impulsive woman who wasn't devious so much as she wanted to be loved, especially by Josh.

Reva was so well-defined from the start that I knew it would be easy and enjoyable to embrace her character—no holds barred. She sounded like fun, and hell, I needed the work. So I kept moving forward with the prospect of playing the part.

My next meeting was a screen test for executive producer Gail Kobe, head writer Pamela Long, and several executives from both Procter & Gamble and CBS. Gail knew my work from *The Doctors* and was very happy that I was interested in playing the part of Reva.

Boy, was Pam Long a big presence. She is a bawdy Southern belle, as well as a former Miss Alabama, and a damn fine actress herself. Earlier in her career, Pamela had appeared for several years on the soap *Texas*. Pam knew how to write for actors because she was one. She knew what kind of material motivated an actor to deliver the best performance, which ultimately helped facilitate her stories. She, like me, had an enormous laugh, and she lit up a room when she walked into it! I eventually forged a wonderful and close working relationship with Pam. I admire her work more than any other writer I've worked with over the years.

Pam beautifully set up Reva's character prior to her arrival by connecting her to Joshua and Billy Lewis through their dialogue. They started talking about Reva four months before she ever showed up.

"Have you heard from Reva?"

"Reva's mad at me."

"Oh, you don't want Reva mad at you!"

"I wonder what Reva is up to."

And so on.

These lines were sporadically dropped into the dialogue as if the audience should already know who Reva was—except they didn't.

By the time Reva appeared in Springfield, the fans were eager to meet the wild girl from Tulsa. With the help of Pam and her writing partners, Jeff Ryder and Jay Hammer, the character blew into town like a tornado, and the fans knew they were in for a wild ride.

My first audition scene was with Jordan Clarke, the actor who played Billy Lewis. We played it full of spit and vinegar. The scene was very well written, and playing it was like a tennis match—I hit a great shot, and Jordan returned that shot with an even better one right down the line! I like to think I won Jordan's respect that day. I know he liked me and told me many years later that he let it be known to the big shots making the decision that I was Reva Shayne.

My next audition scene was with Robert Newman, who played Joshua Lewis. Although I came across as cool, calm, and collected, I was actually a nervous wreck inside, because I wasn't sure I really wanted to do another soap, or whether I should take the job if it was offered. I worried about the audition itself too, because I was going to read with two very established characters on the show, and I knew there were ten other very qualified actresses trying out for the same part.

Robert was four years younger than me and incredibly handsome. Even though he carried a lot of leading man attitude, I sensed some vulnerability in him as well. It was that combination of sexuality and sensitivity that gave his character such range as a daytime "hunk."

My audition with Robert clicked on all cylinders; I felt as if we'd already worked together for years! Though I had a pretty good feeling that Jordan loved me, Robert was very guarded and more difficult to read. Robert was an established, young, gorgeous actor who didn't seem all that interested in Kim Zimmer to play Reva. He played his cards close to the chest. I had no idea what to think of that, because normally I could break through most anyone's walls.

After testing with the actors who would be my leading men and then spending the day with the crew at *Guiding Light*, I had my heart completely set on getting the part. I thought I was perfect for the role, but I had some pretty stiff competition to beat out before the job could be mine. The other women who tested for the role of Reva ran the gamut. Although some were younger, most of the actresses were much older than me, and we were all physically very different. There were two blondes, three redheads, and three brunettes. Some were taller, some shorter. There wasn't a specific look for Reva so much as a personality they were seeking. This was going to be a great role, and every one of us knew it.

I later found out from Jordan and Robert that, as I suspected, I was not Pam's first choice for the character. It turned out she wanted Reva to be a fiery redhead with a Southern accent. Hey, I was a fiery blonde from Michigan—that ain't chopped liver! To her credit, once Pamela saw my chemistry with Jordan and Robert, she changed her mind. Needless to say, I was completely overjoyed when two days later I was cast as the hell-raising "Slut of Springfield"! By November of 1983, I had a contract to play the part of Reva for the next three years.

CHAPTER FIVE

Guiding Light: The Early Days

When Reva finally made her debut, she was probably a little hard to take in the beginning. I chose to play her bigger than life. Yeah, she had big hair, wore big earrings, sported giant Norma Kamali shoulder pads (remember those?), and wore big furs—and it was real fur at that! Everything about Reva was big—especially the day she arrived in Springfield.

My wardrobe consisted of a bath towel and a turban. Not a stitch of clothing more! In the scene, I was being massaged by a very nervous actor playing a masseur, who put so much oil on my back that he couldn't even keep his hands on me. When he rubbed my back his hands would slip right off. Anyway, just as Reva is settling in, Alan Spaulding, played at the time by Chris Bernau, walks through the door of the hotel where he's set Reva up. Like any supposed gold digger, Reva insisted on only the best accommodations, and Alan provides.

Alan has brought Reva to town to break up Billy and Vanessa's engagement. He wants Vanessa all to himself, both in the bedroom and the boardroom. Billy and Reva had been married briefly before Billy left Tulsa to move to Springfield, after supposedly getting a divorce. But Alan has offered Reva a boatload of money to make Billy believe that they're still married and that she's having second thoughts about ever giving him a divorce.

This would make it impossible for Billy and Vanessa to marry, and Alan would have a chance to move in on Vanessa.

Reva was an immediate hit, because the show had been lacking in the bad-girl department. All good dramatic television has to have a villain—and Reva filled that void. Fans loved her and loved to hate her. It was a win-win for everyone, because ratings began to improve and the Lewis family story unfolded into one of the most dominant in the show's history. I think the initial success of the character was due to the strong relationship between head writer, Pam Long, and me.

It didn't take long for me to discover that Reva belonged to Pam Long as much as she did to me. Pam lived vicariously through Reva. Pam and I both have very strong personalities and were always clear about what we wanted for Reva and then did whatever it took to get it! We loved and respected each other, but boy, oh, boy, could we fight. We had a real love-hate relationship that was like a marriage of sorts. Our arguments were never personal. They were always about Reva and strictly about the best interests of the character.

One unforgettable fight happened in a New York City restaurant. Joe Willmore, our executive producer at the time, Pam, and I were having dinner so we could discuss the direction they were going in with Reva. I really can't remember the exact issue, but an argument escalated between Pam and me to such a boiling point that Joe excused himself from the table, went outside, and threw up! He was so upset that his leading actress and head writer were having such an intense argument that it actually made him sick.

Poor baby.

It was clear that Pam and I both came to love Reva so much that we each fought hard for her. If Pam wanted to do something with Reva that I didn't agree with, I made her convince me that she was right and I was wrong. I trusted her, so when she took a firm stand, I'd always give in. Still, I needed Pam to totally convince me that it was the right decision before I could or would invest in the story line.

By the end of the evening, we had settled our issues and left each other with hearty hugs and kisses. Joe was a little green but he survived. That was the way Pam and I fought. We'd go at it with such great intensity and wouldn't quit until we came up with great results!

Reva became the ultimate collaboration between actress and writer. Pam was the heart and soul of the character, as she was the one who put the words in my mouth. And I was the backbone as well as the "face" of Reva. She was composed of the qualities that both Pam and I brought to the table. Together we made Reva real and brought this wonderful, dynamic, and gigantic fictional character to life.

In fact, all the characters were so well developed and well-defined in the writing that playing the history between them was a snap for all of us: Jordan Clarke, Robert Newman, and myself. Robert and I especially were so in tune with each other that we could read each other's mind and began to guess how the other person would play a scene! For two straight years, I got to spend almost every day together with Robert. In that time, we genuinely fell in love!

No, we didn't have a romantic relationship offscreen.

We fell in love with our two characters. As a result, he and I developed an unshakable bond of trust and respect that I think an actor can experience only by working the schedule we have on a soap opera. I was spending more time on the set with Robert than I was at home with A.C. We definitely had an intimate relationship, but only as professionals.

My relationship with Robert both on and off the screen is one that is so precious and rare in this business. We knew each other so well that we knew when to stay away from each other, when we were having a bad day, when to push a scene to the limit, and when not to push at all. We knew each other's body language and understood how to read the energy we both had.

Working with Robert was a dream because it came so easily. That's not to say that every day was a walk in the park. Believe me, we had our moments. But when we had a disagreement, most of the time it was due to something the writers were making our characters do to each other. One example was when Reva was dying of cancer and the writers used her illness to allow Cassie and Josh to canoodle behind Reva's back. I would get upset whenever I made the mistake of reading the message boards on the Internet to gauge how fans were feeling about this story line. People were enraged that Reva wasn't sharing her illness with her family, and they were also upset with Josh for "diddling" her sister.

I would try to defend my character's actions to Robert, who was having the time of his life playing love scenes with a much younger and very beautiful actress who was totally different from me. He didn't mind the story line, because it was freeing him up to experience someone other than Reva.

I'd go to Robert's dressing room and say, "This is ridiculous. Josh would never be with Cassie."

Robert would say, "Why not? It's human nature. Reva's not paying any attention to Josh. How can you tell me that Josh would never do something like that? You don't play my character. I do!"

It would appear the Josh and Reva were going through the same dilemmas that Robert and Kim were offscreen. Robert and I were so close to our characters that we'd often have heated discussions defending their actions as if they were real. Life would definitely imitate art in those instances.

The emotions we displayed to our fans during some of daytime's most passionate moments were honest and true, born from our trust and love. We made each other better actors! I wish everyone could know Robert, the man, as well as I do. I think most people would be surprised by how funny he is. He could make an observation about something that is so normal and put a spin on it that would be hysterically funny because he had such an off-the-cuff delivery. You couldn't help but laugh when he started going off on something. He was our very own Jack Benny.

Over the course of the show, I had the privilege of watching him mature into an amazing actor, husband, father, spiritual adviser (whenever I needed him), and friend. Robert always knew how to get me to see both sides of things, even when I was dead set against it. He is forever a friend. I hope someone out there in TV Land is smart enough to let us play together again!

Even though I had played two other strong female characters on daytime television before joining the cast of *Guiding Light*, nothing compared to the challenges and complexities of playing Reva. It was definitely *The Perils of Pauline* around there; every day Reva was in some type of perilous situation. My job was to take each unbelievable circumstance and make it believable and real. I was called upon to pull this off on a daily basis, whether it be time traveling, playing a clone, having ESP, marrying every male member of one family and loving each of them equally, or hiding away in the back of a truck full of refugees as we all crossed the border into the United States. These were just some of the story lines I had the privilege to play, as well as the challenge to make them feel, look, and be real for the viewer. The writers had so many men falling in love with Reva over the years that whenever a new actor would come on the show, I'd warn him that his character would be in love with Reva within a week, because, as I often said on the set, "Reva's got a golden pussy!" I seriously made up a song about it to the tune of "I've Got a Golden Ticket," from *Willy Wonka*, that I would sing whenever new meat was on the set.

There were many times I read my script and thought, *Are you kidding me?* Still, this was my job, and I had to play Reva the best I knew how.

When I first started work on *Guiding Light*, the studio was on West Twenty-sixth Street in Manhattan (the same studio that now houses Martha Stewart). These studios were our home away from home. I remember one day when I arrived at the studio at six thirty a.m. to start work, the cast and crew from the day before were just walking out! Now, that was a twenty-four-hour day.

The building itself was a bit like an old and musty dungeon, but the cast still loved to call it our home. The dressing rooms were located on the lower level, along with makeup, hair, wardrobe, and a production supervisor's office that at the time was the party room!

We called it the party room because things went on behind closed doors that were only whispered of. After all, it was the eighties, and people were experimenting with all kinds of things! At one point there were rumors (I never saw it with my own eyes) that one of our young actresses had gotten so wasted one night that she ended up duct-taped to the outside of the office door.

It was on the same floor that Mr. Hy Brown, the owner of the building, had his office. To this day, I can't imagine why he wanted to have his office in the midst of a bunch of crazy theatricals like us! He was an interesting man who was instrumental in keeping the radio dramas alive for as long as he could. Although Mr. Brown married into wealth and was extremely rich, he was also a strict penny-pincher. He often searched the actors' dressing rooms and the makeup rooms to find discarded newspapers so he could clip coupons. I remember Joe Cola, our makeup man, opening his morning paper to read and discovering half of it was missing! We all got a good laugh out of that!

The pranksters in the cast (and there were many) used to glue dollar bills to the carpet in front of Mr. Brown's office, then hide and watch him try to pick the bill up off the floor. They were merciless!

On the second floor were the main entrance and guard desk, and up a flight of stairs were the production offices, casting department, writers' offices, set designers and executive producer's office, and the larger of the two studios we used.

The fourth floor was where the smaller studio was. The

whole building was really an incredible maze of cement, but it was home. We had a lot of furry friends who called it home, too—the mice with whom we shared our dressing rooms.

It was Hy Brown's idea to put sticky paper in all the dressing rooms, which meant that our furry friends would get stuck and die a slow death over the weekend. Sometimes you'd walk into your dressing room in the morning and find these cute little creatures alive, but stuck on this paper that they couldn't break free from. Then the cleaning staff would come in and dispose of them like a snotty tissue. I always threw the sticky paper away in my dressing room before my little friends could meet their demise.

My early days as Reva offered me the opportunity to work with some fantastically talented actors, including Chris Bernau, who was a real ballbuster. Chris lived and breathed his character. He was an amazing actor who scared a lot of the other actors he worked with because all he wanted was to do his scenes, do them right, and then move on. There was seldom any laughter working with Chris. If you did somehow make him laugh, it was the highlight of everyone's day. Let's just say that I made him laugh a lot! He'd give me shit and I'd give it right back to him. Although he probably never admitted it, I like to think Chris enjoyed working with me as much as I enjoyed working with him. I found him to be a wonderful challenge and loved every minute of working together. His death in 1989 was a huge shock. Chris traveled extensively, and although I never really knew for sure, it was rumored that he had caught some terrible bug on one of his exotic journeys. His loss was really painful.

Tina Sloan, who played Nurse Lillian Raines, and who was

on *Guiding Light* even longer than I was, had the dubious honor of playing a character who was always being victimized. Although we didn't work in many scenes together, I became a fan of hers from watching her work on the set.

Tina and I were friends, but we couldn't have been more different. We could have easily played each other's character, but in real life, we were nothing alike. Our birthdays were only one day apart, so as fellow Aquarians, we each had the ability to see the big picture and often agreed on world matters, but we often disagreed on the minute details of everyday living. She was a typical "Upper East Sider," who lived in a beautiful three-bedroom apartment in Manhattan among her very high-society friends. Her husband was very successful, and I always assumed that Tina didn't have to work; she chose to. Anyway, she could never quite get over how I'd take the bus to work instead of having a car and driver.

A.C. and I lived in New York City only until Rachel was two years old. She was the queen of Seventy-fifth Street and Columbus Avenue. A.C. would take her all over the Upper West Side while I was working. Between Central Park (on nice days) and the Museum of Natural History (when it rained), they had an endless playground to explore. By the time she turned two, however, I began to think she should have her own backyard—and maybe her own room instead of sleeping in a porta-crib we kept under our loft bed. For us, that meant moving from our one-bedroom walk-up and settling down in the suburbs.

We eventually were able to save up enough money to think about buying our first house. At the time, I was appearing in a pirate musical called *Nobody Starts Out to Be a Pirate* at the

Whole Theater Company, Olympia Dukakis's theater in Montclair, New Jersey. The wonderful Harve Presnell played the pirate king, while I was playing the queen of the lady pirates. I commuted from New York City to the theater by bus to do the show. After we finished bringing the show down at eleven o'clock in the evening, someone would take me to catch the last bus from Montclair back into Manhattan. I fell in love with Montclair, and I was so comfortable with the commute that I figured it would be an easy transition if we bought a house there or nearby.

A.C. and I would often drive out to Montclair on the weekends. While I did our matinee performance, A.C. drove around to look at houses. He eventually connected with a real estate agent named Heidi Buenger, who became a dear friend. She found us the picture-perfect home in which to raise Rachel. And I would take the bus to and from the set of *Guiding Light* for many years to come.

I am just a girl from Michigan whose family was blue-collar all the way. I worked hard for what I earned. My father worked hard, which instilled that spirit in me at the earliest stage of my life. My mother was a homemaker. My sister worked in an office. We were all big savers who never spent our hard-earned money on things that weren't necessary. It killed Tina that one of the stars of *Guiding Light* was taking the bus—by choice!

Even when I was pregnant or had little babies, I opted for public transportation. I brought my son Max and later Jake to the studio in a backpack. Even the curmudgeons hiding behind their newspapers said, "Good morning," to my babies when we climbed on board. Since it was my choice to live in New Jersey,

I never felt it was the responsibility of the show to get me to work. And besides, I actually enjoyed the ride. I used the time to study my scripts, meditate, or just sleep! I could also do some people watching, one of the greatest experiences an actor can have.

I always considered myself someone who was lucky to work in a job that I loved. I never considered myself to be a star—or a *diva*. *Diva* is a title others bestow on you, whether you like the label or not. And, to be clear, I never liked being called a diva, even though I understood why others might see me that way. I worked hard to make myself like every woman you love and want to be friends with. I wanted to be the girl on the street you could come up to and say hello to like you've bumped into an old friend. And, for many people, the actors who played their favorite characters were like extended family members, because we came into their living rooms five days a week, so they felt they knew us. When I rode the bus, I was just like every other working stiff commuting to the city for work.

Early on, I made a conscious decision that when I wasn't playing Reva, I wanted to be just "Kim." I wanted people to know who *I* was too. That was why I always made a point of introducing myself to every extra, day player, and newbie who came to our set. I wanted to welcome them to the fold, because to me, they were guests in my home. I felt a responsibility to make them feel comfortable. I've heard from many people over the years that they liked working our show because of the ease on the set. We had such a warm and loving atmosphere, especially during my early days on the show.

My parents were always very supportive of my career, and

they had gotten used to seeing me on television for four years on *The Doctors*. But it wasn't until I was on *Guiding Light* that I finally felt like I had arrived—at least to my parents. When I called my mom with the good news, her response was classic: "Good! Now I can start watching *Guiding Light* again!"

Mom stopped watching other shows so she could make sure she never missed an episode of mine. This was in the early days of VCRs, which were very expensive back then. Mom didn't own one at the time, so she had to tune in whenever my episodes aired, which was most of the time.

When I started on the show, I was pretty much working five days a week—a lot for a newcomer. Those in the business call contract roles on soaps "golden handcuffs," because you have the security of steady work but you are locked into doing only that role. It's nice to have a steady gig for the next three years, but it also makes you unavailable for other projects in theater or film, or even guest spots on prime-time shows. It can be done, but it's not easy! So you have to accept being "only" a daytime actor, at least in the beginning. That was exactly how I felt from the start. I loved the idea of becoming Reva Shayne, as well as the security. If I occasionally wished I could try something new, well, the feeling would pass. Once you've been on a show for a while, you get used to the great work and the steady paycheck, so that when your contract comes up for renewal, you sign up all over again because you've gotten spoiled by the job. Thus, golden handcuffs! You're cuffed to the job but it's a great one, so really, who cares?

Whenever we had big party scenes, weddings, funerals, or any other large gathering as part of the story, it meant we were

This picture was taken at John Ball Park Zoo, where sixteen years later I would appear onstage.

With my first boyfriend, Mikey, whom I punched in the nose!

My sister, Karen, got the legs in the family… and I got the big mouth.

Summer of '71, where it all began, doing A Funny Thing Happened on the Way to the Forum with Lowell Siebel.

This is how I looked the summer I met A.C., 1974.

A Midsummer Night's Dream, when I fell for my "ass."

With my mom and sister being wined and dined by the dashing Ricardo Montalban.

With Vic "the Bear" Perillo, my first agent.

Prewedding honeymoon with my honey in Hawaii.

The Happiest Day of My Life.

Our first apartment in New York, in front of the kitchen, where A.C. proposed.

Between takes on the set of *The Doctors* with Jim Storm and Frank Telfer.

May 1983. A.C., Rachel, and me enjoying the cherry blossoms in Central Park.

How I commuted to work in the early days.

With my *One Life to Live* cowboy, Clint Ritchie. What a stud!

Wearing ONLY my white fox coat as Reva in 1983.

Reva and Josh swept away in Hilton Head (although we were supposed to be in Venezuela).

With Larkin Malloy at a preparty I threw for Emmy nominees.

Wearing one of my signature red gowns.

That hair! What was I thinking? Winning m
first Emmy in 1985.

Huggin' on my big ol' teddy bear,
Jordan Clarke.

Robert Newman returned to *Guiding Light* after a two-year absence, on the day Reva was supposed to marry Kyle Sampson.

© Alan G. Locher

Zimmer Family Archive

Behind the scenes at Josh and Reva's first wedding with Robert Newman and Jordan Clarke, 1986.

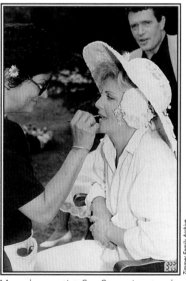

Zimmer Family Archive

My makeup artist, Sue Saccavino, touching me up in between scenes.

My second Emmy win. I had just had Max. Got my Emmy but needed a bra!

© Alan G. Locher

My fave executive producer, Paul Rauch.

© Alan G. Locher

Backstage at the Emmys in 1987 with Robert Newman and Cynthia Watros.

Sue Coflin

That Reva! Always making headlines!

Amish? What do you mean I'm Amish? I'm Reva Shayne!

At the Emmys in 1997 with my adorable husband, who is always by my side.

Dolly, my clone, on her deathbed.

Here's to the ladies who lunch! Front row (*left to right*): Michelle Stafford, Juliette Mills, Kassie DePaiva, Erika Slezak. Back row (*left to right*) Nancy Grahn, me, Martha Byrne, Susan Flannery.

© John Paschal/jpistudios.com

On the set with my favorite director, Bruce Barry.

Zimmer Family Archive

© Alan G. Locher

And my all-time favorite husband on *Guiding Light*, Larry Gates.

Sue Coffin

Family night at the Emmys, 1999, the year of my big loss and Lucci's big win.

On the set of *The Doctors* with two of my favorite mer A.C. and Alec Baldwin, in o youth.

Rachel and me sharing a laugh with Michael Jordan at his celebrity golf tournament in North Carolina, 1999.

Hanging with King Charles: Mr. Barkley at the Jimmy Valvano Charity golf event.

My sister and me putting the squeeze on our daddy!

Big Chill weekend with all my favorite pimps and hos, especially my pimp daddy, A.C.

At the Emmys in 2007. My, how we've grown!

With Sherri Miller, my good friend and creator of the official Kim Zimmer fan club site.

Zimmer Family Archive

Jim Warren

Zimmer Family Archive

Zimmer Family Archive

Skiing with the family at our favorite resort in Taos, New Mexico.

Zimmer Family Archive

After our interview for *60 Minutes* with Morley Safer. What a lovely man.

© *Alan G. Locher*

Zimmer Family Archive

Outdoor concert with my honey at Giants Stadium.

Rockin' out with Bradley Cole for the Red Cross.

Vikki Thompson

Tears and laughter on our last day of shooting. RIP, *GL*!

On stage for "So Long, Springfield" in Pittsburgh.

So Long, Springfield, our final cruise—seriously, it was so windy, we were almost blown off the deck!

looking at a sixteen- to twenty-hour day. These scenes took so long to tape because of the logistics of shooting the entire cast of contract players plus twenty or more extras. Actors with lines had to be seen from several angles, which meant the scene had to be shot over and over from each perspective, with clean views, good lighting, and perfect sound. Technical difficulties were the biggest culprit in slowing things down, so it was a good thing we all liked the studio space. On those particular days, all of the actors planned accordingly by bringing things to do on the set. Usually it meant a stack of crossword puzzles or a good book that you could put in your handbag when you had to be on the set.

Some of the hardest scenes were when your character was sitting in the courtroom observing a trial. We'd always play games in the pews! A cast favorite was "I'm going on a journey and in my suitcase I packed . . ." Each person had to recite what everyone before him packed and then add something to the suitcase. It was great fun and kept us from misbehaving like bad little children!

I felt awful for Jerry verDorn, who played our resident trial attorney on the show, Ross Marler. We'd all be having a great time while he was doing all the work reciting his scads of dialogue. Jerry was always so well prepared. I don't believe I can ever remember a day when he forgot a line and had to stop tape, even though his closing statements on trial days could be anywhere from five to ten pages—a lot of dialogue for one actor.

If the long day spilled into the evening, it usually meant "Chez Phillippe" would be opened for business. Chez Phillippe was Grant Aleksander and Michael O'Leary's shared dressing room, which they decorated in such a cozy, comfy way that it became the actors' lounge. It was the only place you could get one of Grant's superdelicious margaritas! Grant made the absolute best margaritas I have ever had. He never used bottled mix. No, he squeezed fresh limes by hand, making each drink homemade and special. The makeshift bar was eventually closed down by our producers because there were those who took advantage of the situation and returned to the set "toasted."

Oh, I'm not casting stones. Trust me. I showed up on the set toasted more than once toward the end of our run, so I am in no position to judge here.

Aside from the occasional margaritas with Grant and Michael, I kept a small refrigerator in my dressing room, which in the early days used to keep breast milk cold for my babies. I would pump throughout the day at the studio and take the bottles home when we finished shooting. Years later, that same refrigerator came in handy for the occasional bottle of wine I kept in there. You might say that refrigerator went from housing mother's milk to "Mother's" milk. If the day was going past our usual three-o'clock quitting time, I figured it was five o'clock somewhere!

When the writing was on the wall that the show was on its last legs, I began to take my lunch break at Jake's Saloon, a terrific industry bar up the street from the studio. All the local newspeople hung out there, but I considered it my own personal *Cheers* bar, where everyone knew my name. I'd walk through the door and there was always a cold glass of white wine waiting for me. The waitresses were all Irish girls and the waiters were Hispanic. I could rattle off the names of every front-of-the-house employee; they unquestionably took the very best care of me when I stopped in.

I always drank two glasses of wine while I ate my lunch, which was also my biggest meal of the day. Two glasses of wine didn't seem excessive, especially if I was eating a steak or a piece of salmon. It seemed reasonable and certainly something I could handle. The manager always bought me a third glass of wine, however, knowing I wouldn't order one on my own—even if I wanted it—which I did. He never offered to buy me the first two drinks. He knew I would pay for those without batting an eye. But sure enough, he always took care of that third drink.

For a while, especially during the last few years of the show, I was heading over to Jake's three or four days a week. Miraculously, I never went back to the set unable to do my job, though there were plenty of times I'd go back to the studio and have to take a nap before being called to the set. Even if I wasn't able to nap, being a little buzzed made me able to tolerate the rest of my day.

The crew loved when I came to the set after throwing back a few drinks. I'd show up with a determined "let's do this!" attitude. I'd actually say things like "Let's get this scene in the can so we can go home and make mad, passionate love with our real spouses!"

The production crew was my type of people. They were down-to-earth folks who always had my back, even when I was saying things that we all knew would piss off the executives. Our sound guy, Butch, always pointed to my open mic to remind me that everyone in the studio could hear whatever it was that I was saying. This wasn't much of an issue in the early days, because I hardly ever said anything that could get me into hot water. In later years, however, I often vented about my frustration with the show. Butch would try to quiet me down, but I never stopped.

Never.

"Do you think I care what they think? Let them fire me! They need to hear what I have to say, damn it!" I spewed whatever came to my mind out of pure frustration and my growing dissatisfaction with the way things were going.

Okay, looking back, I only went balls to the wall because I was drinking more frequently toward the end of the show. You might even say I was self-medicating. I would have never pulled stunts like that in the early days, or without my liquid courage.

I was so unhappy the last couple of years on the show that I simply didn't care. And to be honest, I think there was a part of me that wanted to get fired so they could put me out of my misery. But I refused to be their scapegoat. If I quit the show, which I thought about numerous times, and the show went off the air, they could blame its demise on my departure. I wasn't about to let that happen. I continued with my liquid lunches so I could put up with the angst and misery during those last few years.

CHAPTER SIX

Memorable Characters

People often ask me about the wonderful talent I have had the pleasure and honor to work with over the years. To be sure, there has been a virtual "who's who" that has come through the doors of *Guiding Light* over the course of its run. But for me there will always be a couple of standout performers whom I loved dearly, with all my heart, and whom I miss each and every day.

In 1984, shortly after I started, Beverlee McKinsey showed up in Springfield as Alexandra Spaulding, and we knew we were in the presence of daytime royalty.

Getting to know Bev was such a joy. She had been the star of *Another World* and then moved her character to the soap *Texas*. The opening credits read, "*Texas*—starring Beverlee McKinsey," which had never been seen before. But if anyone deserved the star billing, Bev did, because she was a consummate professional. Not only was she beautiful—she was also incredibly funny and captivating on camera. She oozed class, even when drinking whiskey and playing poker. Bev was a teeny-tiny woman who carried herself bigger than a giant. Everything that came out of her mouth was a pearl of wisdom. She had a husky, sultry voice, which I figured came from many years of smoking. She was a real *dame*. I aspired to be just like her.

Our characters didn't get along; actually, we were pretty

much at each other's throats, but Beverlee and I always had so much fun working with each other. Often, however, I noticed that she had a hard time remembering her lines whenever we'd do a scene together. I watched her with other actors and she never seemed to have a problem with them. I began to worry that I was doing something to throw her off. I went to her one day and asked if I was doing anything that she found distracting. I was genuinely concerned I was somehow driving her crazy.

"It's not your fault. It's your mom and dad's," she said with a straight face. I was confused, so I asked her to please explain what she meant.

"It's those blue eyes. Whenever I play a scene with you, I get lost in your eyes and all of the dialogue goes out of my head."

You could have bowled me over with a feather when she said that. I admired Beverlee so much, and the idea that she couldn't concentrate when we did a scene was the most precious and beautiful compliment I have ever received.

As much as I respected Beverlee and felt blessed to have had the opportunity to work with her, I always felt that underneath her wit and charm, there was a hurt and angry woman. Maybe *angry* is too harsh a word. But some years later I realized the origin of that curious aura. She simply knew too much! She well understood the nuts and bolts of daytime television and soap operas. As things changed from year to year and creative decisions were made (sometimes by people who had no right to make them), she didn't hold her tongue for anyone. If Bev felt the decisions weren't in the best interest of the show, she would spend her day bitching about them. She knew how things ought to be and how far from the ideal they were. Finally, she simply cut the umbilical cord and left, in a manner that, all these years later, makes all of us who were around say, "Damn, that took balls!"

I was living in California when it all went down, but this is the story I heard.

She had negotiated in her contract to take a month off every year. She took the same month off each year, so there was no surprise in scheduling for the executives or for her. As she was nearing the end of her contract in 1992, no one had come to her to renegotiate. She put in for her month off as usual, except this time, she never came back to work. She had someone come in and clean out her dressing room while she was vacationing. When the suits realized what was happening, they began to panic. No one had talked to her about coming back, so she just up and left. Just like that—she was gone.

Her parting comment to *TV Guide* was "If they're bent out of shape, it's because for once someone beat 'em at their own game!"

It wasn't until I lived through the last two years at *Guiding Light* that I fully got her decision. It was never that Bev was bitter or jealous or bitchy or even diva-esque; she just couldn't tolerate stupidity or naïveté. I can totally appreciate her inability to embrace those qualities, because I would encounter them in the show years later.

Sadly, the world lost Beverlee in 2008 due to complications from a kidney transplant. In a different time and place, she would have been a great executive producer! I would have answered to her in a second! She knew what worked and how to "git 'er done." When I was thinking about titles for this book, I had a conversation with Bev's son, Scott McKinsey. Scott, who had been a director on *Guiding Light* for years and is now a multi-Emmy-winning director on *General Hospital*, told me that Beverlee always wanted to have a certain phrase for her epitaph: "You're standing in my light!" I laughed incredibly hard when Scott told me that, because Beverlee always knew where her light was, and she was never afraid to let you know if you were standing in it. Scott told me he thought that would be a good title for my book! I told him I was honored but I could never live up to that title. Ask any lighting designer I've ever worked with; I never knew where my light was!

I was sorely disappointed that the producers of the Emmys didn't do a tribute to Beverlee the year she died. She surely deserved one. To make matters worse, they actually left her out of the memorial tribute they do each year, which broke my heart. Beverlee McKinsey was a treasure and a legend. I am truly blessed for the years we spent working together and for the friendship we shared offscreen, too.

Another important and huge impact on my life at *Guiding Light* was the actor Michael Zaslow, also known as Roger Thorpe, "the bad guy" on the show. Michael played his treacherous character with such force that you believed he actually was Roger.

He had originated the role back in 1971, and in 1980, when he decided to leave *Guiding Light*, he wanted to make sure there was no possibility of ever being wooed back to the show. He was tired of playing the character and didn't want the temptation of ever coming back, so when Roger Thorpe fell off a jagged cliff to the rocks below, Michael insisted that the camera show his broken and battered body on the rocks so there could be no doubt he was dead! That succeeded in convincing the audience he was never coming back . . . until his unexpected resurrection eight years later.

Michael's return to *Guiding Light* reminded me of the scene in the movie *Soapdish* where Whoopi Goldberg's character reminds the producers of her show that they can't bring back Kevin Klein's character because he had been decapitated. Their response was to give his character the very first successful head transplant. Miracle of miracles, he was now alive and well and being written back into their show! Michael's return to *Guiding Light* was a textbook soap opera move, in that there was no possible way he could have survived his fall off the rocky cliff—but he did.

You see? No one's ever really dead in Soap Land!

Michael was a force to be reckoned with and was very opinionated. In other words, he didn't take shit from anyone. If he didn't like something, he'd let you know. Michael didn't care if he hurt someone's feelings or stepped on toes. He knew who his character was and fought for Roger with everything he had. If a scene was written that made his character any less than who Michael thought he was, Michael would pitch a royal fit until it was fixed to his satisfaction.

As years passed, Michael began suffering from ALS (also known as Lou Gehrig's disease). He started having trouble retaining his dialogue. It was an incredibly difficult time for him, because he was a master at dialogue, loved words and could spin lines like no one else; now suddenly he was losing his ability to do what he loved most.

Everyone was aware that Michael was sick, and it was shocking, at least to me, when *Guiding Light* decided not to renew his contract, which left him both sick *and* without a job. Fortunately, during his first absence from *Guiding Light* he had played another wildly popular character named David Rinaldi, a concert pianist, on *One Life to Live*; he still had a lot of friends at ABC who fortunately did the right thing and hired Michael back on *One Life to Live* so he could continue working throughout his illness. He played David Rinaldi until he was physically no longer able to continue, leaving that show for good in 1997.

I learned so much from Michael and from the courage and strength of his incredible family during his fight against ALS. When Michael became too sick to continue acting, he and his wife, children, and members of his daytime family set up a foundation in his name for ALS research. The foundation regularly organized benefits in order to raise awareness and money for the cause. Michael always made sure to make a personal appearance at the events, even if he was feeling weak. By that time, he'd taken to using a wheelchair and could talk only with the help of a computer-generated voice provided by a DynaVox device.

I can still remember watching the devastation that his sickness wreaked on Michael. He was a strong individual who put up quite a fight until he eventually succumbed to his illness on December 6, 1998. His wife, Susan, their two daughters, and hundreds of people from the daytime community were in attendance at his funeral. I'll never forget the moment his eldest daughter, Marika, walked to the altar with three of her friends from school and played a beautiful concerto on the violin dedicated to his memory. The character Roger Thorpe had nothing on the real man. The love he had for his family, his commitment to his work, and the strength he showed in fighting this disease are who Michael was.

Michael's memorial was full of stories from colleagues from various stages of his career, people he'd worked with in the theater as well as in film and television. The tales were told with incredible humor and touching memories that made us all laugh and cry and would have made Michael smile. He had an immense ego, and it was that very ego that people adored about him; it also gave him the strength he needed to fight that terrible debilitating disease for as long as he did. The memorial service was one of the most moving experiences of my life and reminded me how important it is to make the most of time spent with loved ones. I really miss him.

Sometimes, the most memorable moments you share with a fellow actor don't happen on the set; they happen behind the scenes. Vince Williams played a character named Hampton Speakes, an old football buddy of Billy Lewis's who came to town to help Billy open the Heartbreaker bar. The chemistry between "Hamp" and Reva was okay, but between Kim and Vince, it was gold.

Although he was on the show for only a short time, Vince and I became fast friends. He was one of the nicest and gentlest men I have ever known. I never heard him say an unkind word about anyone. He was an exceptional actor and human being and a very talented saxophonist too.

When I decided to leave *Guiding Light* in 1990, I threw myself a going-away party for the cast and crew. Everyone came to see me off, including Vince, who brought his saxophone that night. As a going-away gift to me, Vince played the most moving and rich version of Joe Cocker's "You Are So Beautiful" I have ever heard. The room was silent except for the sultry sound of Vince's sax, which was fortunately muffling the sounds of my sobs as he played. It was the best gift ever. I didn't know it then, but that was the last time I would ever see Vince. He got very sick with a fast-moving cancer and died shortly after I moved to Los Angeles. I can still hear the sound of his sax whenever I close my eyes and think of him.

And who could ever forget the exquisite mother to all, Charita Bauer, who played Bert Bauer? I don't know how they ended up with the same last name! Let's talk about soap opera names for a minute . . . Ridge, Thorn, Rip, Reva, Meta, and Roxy, just to name a few. Where do these names come from? I happen to know that on our show, a lot of the names came from writers wanting to immortalize favorite people in their lives. They would name characters after their aunts, uncles, the boy they were in love with in middle school, the boy who never asked them out on a date, or the girl who shut them down. For the most part, the character names were personal to the writers. However, there were the occasional names that came from the show. For example, Reva's daughter, Marah, was named for two characters on the show: Josh's mother, Miss Martha, and Reva's mother, Sarah. Put the names together and you've got yourself a Marah.

Anyway, I'd heard many stories about Charita Bauer before I even started on the show. She was, after all, the grande dame of *Guiding Light*.

When I started the show in 1983, Charita had actually lost a foot due to a blood clot from circulatory problems. The writers decided to mirror her true life story by having Bert lose a leg. She became a mentor to Robert when Josh became paralyzed after a car accident. I often watched her on the set help him tap into his character's emotional crisis, offering suggestions as to how to play the scenes in an authentic way as someone who no longer had the use of his legs. It was the old guard teaching the new regime.

I never had the honor to work with Charita, as she became too ill to work shortly after my arrival in Springfield and eventually passed away about a year after that. Robert often shared stories with me about what it meant to him to have Charita guide him through that story when she herself was struggling.

Most of the people I have chosen to single out in my book have been salt-of-the-earth individuals. But let's face it: Not everyone I worked with over the years fits that description. A soap opera cast is like a family. And, as with all families, there will be an occasional troublemaker, black sheep, or outcast who doesn't last that long before being exiled—and in the case of a soap actor, that means the unemployment line.

There was one actress who fell in love with all of her costars. Really. She seriously fell hook, line, and sinker on several occasions. And the actors who were the objects of her affection were all too happy to oblige. She fell in love with one costar while she was still married, eventually divorced her husband, and moved in with the costar. For whatever reasons, that relationship didn't last. Her next conquest was another costar who was married—as was she, having gotten married . . . again . . . but this time to someone outside the business. She ended up leaving her husband for this guy; the two actors had decided they were both going to get out of their relationships so they could be together. Unfortunately for her, he got cold feet and never left his wife. For the first time since I knew her, she was suddenly neither married nor involved. Hell hath no fury like a woman scorned!

This actress was miserable on the set, off the set, on the street, in the movies, at the grocery store, and everywhere she went for a very long time. Her presence on the set was a dark energy until she eventually left the show. I was really sorry to see her go, because the show suffered from the loss of her character—and, to be honest, I really liked her, because she had balls the size of those on the statue of David!

Through everything that happens in front of the cameras and behind the cameras, what made *Guiding Light* so special was the quality of the talent that passed through those doors year after year. I got so much joy out of working with each one of these people. They made going to work fun, interesting, and something to look forward to each day. They became my other family, and I will forever be grateful for the many years and memories we all shared.

CHAPTER SEVEN

The Family Business

Daytime television is notorious for creating hard-to-believe, larger-than-life story lines that seem to go on and on. One of these is the length of time a pregnancy can last. For story reasons, a character might be pregnant for eleven or twelve—or fourteen—months! Other times it seems hardly three months pass between a character discovering she's pregnant and the dramatic delivery.

I became pregnant with my second child in 1986, and the writers made my character pregnant too. This time, the story involved Reva's life being threatened, so the writers sent her into hiding for three months while I was on maternity leave. Before leaving, I went to the powers that be and told them that I'd take a shorter maternity leave if they would allow me to bring my new baby to work after he was born. I knew I'd be nursing like I did with Rachel and would want Max at the studio with me during the day.

I delivered Max on March 17, 1987. But when I came back to work, Reva was still pregnant. I had to strap on the pregnancy pillow and carry that faux belly around for three more months until she gave birth. The upshot to this story line was that I could lose all of my baby weight, drop my TV baby, and immediately be in prepregnancy shape again! Haven't you wondered how celebrities pull that off?

I was thankful the producers agreed to allow me to bring Max in with me, much to the dismay of Chris Bernau, whose dressing room was two doors down from mine. By the time I returned to work, I had hired a nanny named Trudy, who met me every morning at the studio so she could watch Max while I was on the set. She was only eighteen years old when she started, and she remained with us for the next twenty years.

Being a single man with no children, Chris thought the idea of bringing children to work was ridiculous. He was worried that the baby would disrupt the peace and quiet of the dressing room area. I guess he had no idea that babies sleep a lot!

One of my favorite memories of Chris was an afternoon when Max was sleeping. Trudy had slipped out to get lunch while I was getting my makeup done right down the hall. I had left Max asleep in the dressing room. When I returned, I found Chris with Max in his arms and he was cooing to him! I'm serious. It seems Max woke up crying. Much to my surprise, Chris went into my room and picked him up. He didn't come and get me; he wanted to settle Max himself. I was so touched by Chris that day and realized there was a lot more to this man than just that grumpy actor who hated kids. He was kind and gentle and would have been an amazing father. From that day forward, I never saw Chris in the same way.

After I had Max, the producers at *Guiding Light* asked if I would like to use him as "baby Marah" on the show. It made sense because they knew he'd be on the set anyway. After mulling the offer over, I discussed it with A.C., and we decided that even though his salary for the show would have enabled us to start a nice little college fund, we didn't feel comfortable using him. I would have felt awful if in the middle of a scene he started fussing or had a poopy diaper or didn't like Robert Newman, his TV dad. In the end, it would have been too much of a distraction. Besides, through my experience in daytime television, I've learned that it is easier to pass a fussy baby off to a show baby wrangler rather than have that baby wrangler be me!

However, months later I did end up allowing Max to fill in one day in a pinch. He made his official television debut when the twin girls who were hired to play baby Marah got sick and weren't able to make it in for the day. Since all of the scenes were with me anyway, I agreed to allow Max to make this onetime appearance. There was only one drawback: Since we had to match the outfit that baby Marah had been wearing the day before, Max was dressed in a lacy pink footed sleeper. Even though the scenes played beautifully, I'm sure Max will never forgive me for dressing him up as a girl that day!

Max wasn't my only child to be featured on the show. When the producers were looking for a young girl who resembled the character of Jessie Matthews for a flashback scene, I offered up my daughter, Rachel, to use as "baby Jessie." At three years old, Rachel looked very much like her. All Rachel had to do was sit on the lap of the actress playing her mother in the scene while she read her a story. Simple enough, right?

Well, maybe for Rachel, but not so easy for the actress playing her mother. She had a tendency to be a bit nervous and anxious on any given day, but when you added a three-year-old to the mix, there was potential for disaster.

Children have an innate sense of danger and can usually detect discomfort in other people. Rachel wanted nothing to do with the actress holding her, much less being a TV star! She pitched a major fit and was unable to do the scene!

It was a good thing that A.C. had accompanied me to work that day to serve as the baby wrangler, because I was busy shooting my scenes. He tried everything to calm our daughter down. He even sat under the desk out of sight of the camera so that only Rachel could see him. But still, no dice! Bruce Barry, the director, tried bribing Rachel with promises of a shopping spree at Toys R Us! But nothing worked. Finally, after twenty minutes of angst and anxiety, A.C. wisely pulled the plug on the whole thing. Bruce agreed that it wasn't worth the trauma to the poor kid, and the scene was rewritten without a "baby Jessie."

In a funny twist, the next time I was pregnant, with my son Jake, Reva was also pregnant, but this time she gave birth *before* I did, which meant I had to do labor scenes while still pregnant—making birth twice as fun. Even though I had given birth twice, feigning labor was really difficult! I was afraid I would hurt myself or my unborn baby by grunting and moaning. I wanted to play the scenes as close to real as I could; I think it's important to make my work look realistic. Even so, when it came time for Reva to deliver, I backed off a bit on my TV labor so I wouldn't accidentally go into real labor!

Yes, this was typical of the strange and sometimes comingled life of a daytime diva and the character she plays on television.

Several years later, my lifelong friend Alan Locher, who was the vice president of publicity for TeleNext at the time, alerted me that there were going to be some upcoming scenes in the show that called for a thirteen-year-old boy to act opposite Reva Shayne. He said he had the perfect young boy in mind.

Alan knew my son Jake had developed an interest in acting. By the time he was thirteen years old, Jake had already played Mercutio in *Romeo and Juliet* and the dentist in *Little Shop of Horrors* at his junior high. The casting director agreed with Alan and thought it would be a great publicity stunt to use Kim Zimmer's real son in those scenes. Ah, nepotism! Ya gotta love it!

As you can imagine by now, I had a slightly different take on the situation.

Yes, it would have been great to have the opportunity to act with my wonderful son, but at the same time I also wanted him to experience the audition process without the helping hand of Mom. It was important to me that Jake audition for the role like any other thirteen-year-old so that he learned what it took to be awarded a part in the business. And wouldn't you know it—he ended up getting the part! And, if I do say so myself, my son happened to be quite good.

There was no doubt that the acting bug had bitten him. All Jake wanted for Christmas that year was an agent and decent head shots! So by fourteen, he'd landed an agent, gotten head shots, and never looked back. To this day, Jake continues to work in the industry. It's a tough business, but he is hanging in there. I couldn't be prouder of him!

There were many times when my real life blended with my television life, and oftentimes my television life felt all too familiar. Let me tell you, it's not easy living with, let alone being married to, someone whose job requires being in relationships with other men all the time. It takes a strong man with intensely good self-esteem and confidence to stand by and watch that unfold.

There were plenty of days and nights when I spent more time

with my on-screen lovers, husbands, boyfriends, and love interests than I did with my own husband. I truly loved the primary characters in my daytime life. I was in love with most of them—whoa. I know what you're thinking, but I don't mean *love* as in anything ever happened. What I mean is that I genuinely loved these men as people, admired them as actors, and loved that I got to *love* them. Did I ever fantasize about being with any of them? Well, I didn't have to, because my job was to love them—every day. And really, who could blame me? They were each handsome, sexy, and very appealing.

Robert Newman was single when I first came on the scene and he'd often want to go out and have drinks after the show. I was newly married with a young baby at home, but I was always game. Even though I loved going home at the end of the day to A.C. and Rachel, it was also fun to go out and flirt with the handsome actor playing the love of my life. Looking back, I should have made a beeline for home, but I didn't. I was addicted to the work. I spent so many hours in the studio with the people I worked with, especially those with whom I shared scenes. We'd sometimes finish our days as late as ten o'clock at night. I guess you could say I had two families: the one I had at home and the one I shared on the set. Weekends were reserved for A.C. and the kids—but weekdays belonged to *Guiding Light*.

There were times my husband and I would argue over my decisions to stay late at work. He wanted me to be home, to be *his* wife. Deep down, I understood what he was saying. I didn't want to hurt him, but I didn't want to give up the joy I felt when I was working.

Our policy has always been to never go to bed angry. Let me

tell you, this is a good mantra for any marriage. A.C. has always had the ability to make me laugh, so if things were getting heated between us, he'd do something to break the ice. Before we knew it, we were both cracking up and forgetting what we were fighting about in the first place.

One of those fights took place during my first few years on the show. Reva had really taken off and was an enormously popular character. As a result, my time at home was extremely limited. In addition to shooting the show, working intense hours five days a week, I was also doing photo shoots, interviews, publicity, and anything else the suits asked me to do. Add weekend publicity junkets in shopping malls all over the country to the equation and you can probably figure out that I was never home.

My contract called for me to go on these junkets, do autograph-signing sessions, publicize the show, and meet the fans. But needless to say, A.C. was feeling neglected, and he wasn't holding back about it. I was furious with him. I couldn't believe he didn't understand that these trips were part of my job.

"If it weren't for this job, we wouldn't have this house, our cars, and all of the other things around here my job pays for!" I was on a real rant. I began chasing him around the pool table in our family room, my blood boiling. That was when he picked up our son Max, who was a toddler, and held him up in front of his body like a shield so I couldn't get to him. In that moment, I realized how ridiculous I was acting. We both broke down and laughed so hard, we had tears streaming down our cheeks. My husband is the funniest man I know!

While I was the primary breadwinner while doing *The Doctors* and the early years on *Guiding Light*, I have always had the

utmost respect for my husband. He has always been able to provide for our family, and was the sole breadwinner many times
himself over the years. Our partnership has been one that has
allowed each of us to pursue our passions regardless of the paycheck. We've both worked throughout our relationship, especially when we lived in New York.

I even had the good fortune of working *with* my husband
when he was directing for a time at *Guiding Light*. I knew from
watching other things he had directed that he had the ability to
pull a performance out of a rock if need be. He was a genius
with actors.

Of course, sometimes you have to play hardball. I remember
being in the rehearsal hall one day while A.C. was working
through a scene with a young actor who kept complaining that
his dialogue was complete garbage. When the actor was finished
venting, A.C. simply said to him, "If you want Shakespeare, go
work off-off-Broadway for peanuts! If you like the money this
job affords you, then get your head out of your ass and do the
job you're being well paid to do here!" To be honest, I wanted to
stand up and applaud!

A.C. was what we call an "actor's director," and he was and
still is the best. But now he was going to have to direct the
"diva" of *Guiding Light*, who also happened to be his wife!

Good luck with that.

On the day that A.C. was calling the shots, I had a very long
monologue. Somehow, he got it in his head that he wanted it to
be one continuous tracking shot—no edits, no cutaways. That
meant there would be no pickup spots. Pickup spots are places
where an edit can be made if an actor forgets his or her lines or

a camera screws up—places where there's a natural cutaway to another actor who may be speaking or reacting. A.C. wanted to capture my scene in one shot! I could have killed him. But he knew how much I loved a challenge, so it was game on!

Well, we got that scene in one take! The man's a genius; what else can I say? He knows me so well that he was certain I could pull off the scene and do it his way. I wish we had been given more opportunities to work together over the years. I love his mind and the way he knows how to see things before they happen. Being that tuned in is what makes my husband a wonderful director and, to be honest, a fantastic husband.

CHAPTER EIGHT

Leaving *Guiding Light* . . . the First Time

Soon after our son Jake was born in 1990, I realized that my family was more important to me than my career. I was spending so much time away from home, missing out on all of those milestones that both parents should experience. In addition, I thought it was time to give A.C. the chance to get back to pursuing his dreams of acting and teaching. He was offered a position at the California Institute of the Arts. It was a well-respected arts conservatory, and he would be teaching everything he loved: acting, directing, and stage combat. I couldn't deny him this chance to do something I knew would be so meaningful and important to him, and I was ready to try something new and spend time with my young family, so I made the decision to leave *Guiding Light*. I had been on the show for seven years and my contract was up, so it seemed like a good time to leave. As an actress, I was also ready for a change of scenery. I wasn't sure what that meant, but I knew I wanted to leave *Guiding Light*. When I told the producers about my decision, they were very understanding and assured me that the door would always be open in the event I chose to return. They couldn't have made it an easier transition for me, and I was very appreciative of how it went down.

My character was written out of the show after Josh took Reva to Florida for a rest. She was suffering from postpartum depression and accidentally drove her car off a bridge and into the Atlantic Ocean. Even though Josh never gave up his search for the body, Reva was presumed dead. With that plunge into the water, I was free to pursue other goals and aspirations. Much to my surprise, fans accepted my decision to leave the show. They hated to see Reva leave but made it apparent they didn't want to see her recast. That type of support gave me some assurance that the producers would have a hard time if they disappointed the fans by trying to recast the role with another actress. I wanted to believe that attempting to recast Reva would have been a terrible failure. Thank God we never had to find out!

We moved our entire brood to Valencia, California. A.C.'s office was right down the street from our new home. I brought the kids to see him almost every day so we could all have lunch together. It made me feel good inside knowing he was doing something that made him so happy. And, boy, was he a big shot on campus. All the young coeds had crushes on him.

Once we got settled, I was offered a role on the short-lived daytime drama *Santa Barbara*. I was brought in to be A Martinez's new love interest by Pam Long, the writer who'd created the role of Reva Shayne on *Guiding Light*, and Paul Rauch, my all-time favorite executive producer. It was mostly because of Paul that I was so happy to be asked to join the cast. I had met him on occasion but had never had the good fortune of being able to say I'd worked for him.

Paul was tough, acerbic, short-tempered, and demanding, but he was also appreciative of talent, explicit about what he liked and didn't like, had a wicked sense of humor, and above all else (though I know some would disagree), he was kind. He knew exactly what he wanted out of his shows and their actors, and worked like a dog to get it! Paul was old-school soap opera. He loved beautiful sets, costumes, lighting, and locations to shoot in. He loved going to exotic places all over the globe and shooting romance and intrigue in a location that the fans could fantasize about being in too. This was in the 1980s and early 1990s, when the soaps had money to burn, and before all of the travel shows on cable existed that let viewers see the world vicariously. The soaps that Paul Rauch produced gave the fans all of that! I adore this man and hope to someday work for him again.

I was brought in to give their show a boost to their slacking ratings. In the meantime, Marcy Walker, who had played A's love interest on *Santa Barbara*, had been hired by *Guiding Light* to be the new love interest for Josh. In the end, the switcheroo didn't work. The audiences didn't accept either of us in our new roles.

One thing I know for sure is that no one person should have to carry the burden of a show's success (or failure) on his or her shoulders when it is an ensemble cast. It is a terrible weight to carry around. My job on *Santa Barbara* lasted only eight months. Word had come down that the show had been canceled and was being taken off the air.

Even though I was there for only a short time, it was sad to experience the cancellation. Anytime a production comes to an end, it's like a breakup. People were walking around the hallways of the studio stunned by the news, talking to their agents and managers, trying to find another job. I hadn't been on the show long enough to be devastated by its demise. I looked at the news as an opportunity to catch up on lost time with my family, and an opening to pursue other roles I could find only in Hollywood.

I did a lot of guest appearances on television shows during that time, including *MacGyver, Models Inc., Babylon 5*, and even an episode of *Seinfeld*. I didn't give up on acting so much as I had burned out from the daily grind of working in daytime. Still, I missed *Guiding Light*—a lot.

The five years we lived in Los Angeles, 1990 to 1995, were during a time I think of as our five years in hell. Everything seemed to be going wrong in California, including mudslides, brush fires, the Northridge earthquake, the O. J. Simpson trial, and the Rodney King riots. Thank God we had incredible friends whom we grew to depend on for our fun and entertainment! Much like our lifelong friends in New York, we had a crazy, fun-loving, game-playing group of party-hearty friends in Los Angeles, who made those years somewhat tolerable. To this day, no matter where our lives have taken us, we all gather every September at the home of my favorite "hostess with the mostest," Cathy Ann Girvan, and her husband, Garrett, for a weekend we refer to as our Big Chill! It always includes a theme party where everyone dresses up in elaborate costumes for one of the evenings. Past years have included everything from pimps and whores to pirates to a safari theme!

The weekend is three days of good food, great California wine, tennis, boccie ball, swimming, sing-alongs, and, of course, our favorite, Butt Darts—a game we usually play in shorts or a bathing suit. You place a quarter between your butt checks and maneuver around an obstacle course set up around the swimming pool and then drop the quarter into various cups of water. The first one to make it around the course, hitting all of the cups with their quarter, wins the coveted golden butt cheek award! This is our answer to *The Lost Weekend*, and one we all look forward to every year!

Despite the fun times with friends, it was the Northridge quake that finally pushed me over the edge to leave California. I didn't want to live in fear of the ground beneath my feet suddenly dropping away. I certainly didn't want my children to live like that. I'd had it. I was ready to get back to New York and to *Guiding Light*—that is, if they would have me.

I made the dreaded phone call to Ed Trach, the executive who was in charge of the show for Procter & Gamble at the time. I was so nervous he would slam down the phone when he heard my voice. After all, my character had been killed off the show. But, as we all know, that didn't mean she was dead!

When Ed answered, I closed my eyes and jumped right in with what I had to say. "I know Reva is dead, but if you have any interest in resurrecting her, I am more than ready to come back to the East Coast." I didn't want to sound like I was groveling, but I am sure he could tell I was nervous by my shaky voice and soft, humble tone.

"We would have you back in a second if you're ready to come back to us!" Ed said.

I have to admit that his warm response made me feel really good. I wasn't getting the same kind of reception in California. I worked a lot while I was there, but I never bonded with any of those jobs like I did with my role on *Guiding Light*. A.C. and I were excited about going home to Montclair, New Jersey. We called Heidi Buenger, our favorite real estate broker, and told her the good news. We bought the first house she showed us. Like Neil Diamond says, "L.A.'s fine, but it ain't home!" We were so happy to be heading back to the East Coast.

Good-bye, L.A.; hello, Springfield. It was time to come back from the dead and reprise my role as Reva—sort of.

Reva's return to *Guiding Light* consisted of her waking up from a long coma to find herself with amnesia, living in Amish country. She was now going by the name Rebecca. Hey, I don't make this stuff up!

CHAPTER NINE

Backstage Pass

Ask any actor who works in daytime and they'll most likely tell you that the hair and makeup rooms are the main hubs of activity. Every morning, before anything else, the actors spend an hour or more in these rooms being painted, teased, trimmed, plucked, and blown. (No, not what you are thinking, although I'm sure there have been exceptions—but none I am privy to!)

Our makeup and hair rooms were truly where life happened for the cast. When we leaned back in our chairs every morning, it was almost as if we were in a therapist's office. Because of the strong relationships we built with the hair and makeup people, the room became a confessional. Secrets were divulged in whispers, drama unfolded, and people announced engagements, pregnancies, affairs, and divorces. Over time, those two rooms were where everyone felt at ease and allowed themselves to get everything off their chest.

On any given day, *Guiding Light* had three full-time staff members whose sole job was to oversee hair and makeup for the actors on our show. All of these people were true artists in their field and all were absolute magic makers. Together, I considered *Guiding Light*'s hair and makeup team our "beauty Mafia."

Seriously.

Check out these names: Cola, Saccavino, Stanzione, Librizzi, and Gebbia. I swear, you had to be Italian to work in that union!

As good as each and every one of them was, and they were all terrific, cast members had favorites. Every morning, it was basically a race to see who could get into the chairs first. I knew that some studio makeup rooms had a hierarchy, and those actors who had seniority got their choice. Well, that wasn't the case for our show. Everyone was created equal, and it was first come, first served. If you got there late, you had to wait around to get your makeup done. The only exception was if you were next up on the set. Then and only then were you allowed to bypass the line. There were plenty of times I was patiently waiting for my turn when another actress would blow in late for her call and be needed on the set. Of course, I had to let whoever it was go ahead of me because she was up first—meaning her scenes were shooting before mine.

One of my favorite makeup artists was Joe Cola. I loved Joe to death, and my morning time in his chair always included his stupid joke of the day (he wrote joke books, in fact). Some of them were pretty dirty, but we all enjoyed them! I pretty much split my time between Joe and Sue Saccavino.

The "look" in the 1980s was all about the eyes, and Sue really knew mine. When I was pregnant, Sue was a master at doing my entire face while I was somehow able to squeeze in a good twenty-minute power nap in her chair. When she was finished, I'd feel a gentle tap on my shoulder and hear Sue whisper, "Wake up. It's time for mascara." It was just too difficult to curl my lashes and apply mascara with my eyes closed, but if she could have, I am certain she would have!

My two favorite hairstylists were Linda Librizzi and Ralph Stanzione. In fact, Linda still cuts my hair to this day. She knows every strand on my head personally, cowlicks and all. In the thirty-plus years I've known Linda, I've probably had another stylist touch my hair four times—if that. I do get my color done by Maria in Montclair (for half the price I'd pay in Manhattan), but other than that, no one touches these tresses.

Over the course of my career on the show, my hair went through a lot with Linda. Whenever she was having a fight with her husband or was upset with production, Linda made sure my hair paid for it with heavy-duty yanking, pulling, and teasing. But all I had to say was "Hey, it's me! Go easy!" and she'd laugh and go about her business. But if she offered to cut my hair on one of those days, I usually told her that it could wait a day . . . or two!

I was famous for getting bored with my hairstyles, so I was constantly changing them up. I'd adjust the color and cut, go short or add extensions. Linda loved creating new looks for me. It seemed like every six months we'd change the style up with a new cut or color. Every time we did, Linda got calls from people all over the country wanting to fly to New York to have her give them a custom "Reva cut."

As on most soaps, the general policy on the show was not to change your look without getting permission. You'd have to go to the executives and explain why you wanted a new look. Sometimes they'd say yes and other times no. Some of them, like Paul Rauch, our executive producer from 1996 to 2002, really hated it when actors changed their look, because he believed the fans knew us with a certain appearance. Of course, Paul was pretty extreme; he even discouraged the occasional ponytail. He liked the women on his shows to look feminine and beautiful all the time!

Ralph Stanzione was wonderful at creating the perfect party updos and wedding hair. Although he was a good stylist, I believe his real calling was wardrobe. Ralph knew exactly what he liked and had no problem telling people what he didn't. He made it his business to go down to the wardrobe room every morning to see what I would be wearing so he could either rave about the choice or warn me that I should save some time by going in there to check it out before showtime. Ralph was an impeccable dresser and had a wonderful sense of style, so I trusted his opinions. Reva Shayne had a strong sense of style; Kim Zimmer, not so much!

In the early days, characters on the show were impeccably dressed, because the budget for wardrobe was endless. I can remember putting on seven-hundred-dollar silk blouses, four-hundred-dollar slacks, expensive designer jewelry, and loads of real furs worth thousands of dollars. Reva's favorite fur coat happened to be a Christie Brothers white fox. At the time, my favorite fragrance was Estée Lauder's White Linen, which I wore all the time—so that meant Reva wore it too. Since the show didn't own the furs, they were borrowed, then returned to the vaults at Christie Brothers every night. Whenever they were needed, the furrier said my coats were the easiest to find because he'd follow his nose to the White Linen.

Giving tours of the wardrobe room was always fun, because visitors could always pick out whose racks of clothing belonged to what character with ease. Each character was so well-defined in what he or she wore, it was very simple to figure out. For example, Reva wore lots of white, Josh wore jeans and flannel shirts, H.B. always had his ten-gallon Stetson cowboy hat and boots, and Mindy always had her expensive designer clothing in polka dots and pastels.

When I returned to the show after a five-year hiatus, not much had changed, except the budget for wardrobe had been slashed and we had two new makeup people. There was Paul Gebbia, whom I knew from my brief stint at *One Life to Live*, and Helen Gallagher. Helen was the life of the party in the makeup room. She was a fiery redhead before she decided to go au naturel by letting her hair go gray, and dubbed herself our "makeup slave." (Or maybe she just used that phrase with me.) Helen was also everyone's high priestess. She studied astrology and crystals and knew how to read people's energy. She memorized everyone's astrological signs. She always offered her insights but never forced them on you.

The cast tended to confide in her about everything because she was such an incredible listener. Over time, I guess she had to be. After all, Helen was stuck with us crazy actors in her chair for thirty-five minutes each and every day! I can't imagine what it must have been like for her at the end of the day after listening to all the screwy actors and advising them about their problems. She used to say that she was building her karma for her next life. I began to think of her as my mama guru.

On Fridays, Helen cranked up her little boom box at her station with whatever rock-and-roll music she had that day and gave me my TGIF "boogie down" makeup job! Let me tell you, that girl could boogie with the best of them. She was funny,

funny, funny—like a character Tracey Ullman would create in one of her shows. Her laugh was penetrating and even a little contagious. I can't even count the number of times we cracked each other up and fell into uncontrollable laughing jags. I'm sure it was more than annoying to anyone within earshot.

Before we had an actual Peapack location, the show started shooting on various locations in the town of Peapack, New Jersey. Whenever we were out and about, the show didn't provide honey wagons—a place for us to pee—or trailers we could use between scenes to stretch, prepare for our next scene, or kill time (which could be upward of three hours) waiting to be called to the set. As you can imagine, the designated hair and makeup room was even more important as a central gathering place, because it was the only place we could go!

Working on the show in Peapack was like being part of some high school senior film project (maybe not even that good!). It did gradually get better with time, especially after we got the actual Peapack show house, but in the beginning we sometimes had to change in public restrooms because the producers didn't want to take the time to drive back to our base camp. It took one time of standing naked in a public restroom at a bank when I came face-to-face with a fan who commented on how nice it was to "see" me, before I said, "Okay! I won't do this anymore!" That was when the producers told me they were working on getting a production house to use. They promised me things would get better when that happened. And they did. We still had no individual dressing rooms and very little privacy. Thank God we all liked one another so much, because we had to share bathrooms too! And we all know how stinky boys can be. In fact, there was one actor who stopped at a local convenience store on the way to Peapack every morning to pick up his morning cup o' joe and drop off his morning "deposit" so he wouldn't have to do it in the show house.

All of the rooms in the production house were typically used as sets, and some days we weren't allowed to be in them because they were "hot sets," meaning they had to match exactly from the day before, so nothing could be touched or moved. On other days, when a room wasn't being used, we could stretch out and chill while the show was being shot elsewhere in the house. Even so, we had to be quiet as church mice while shooting was going on—we couldn't walk around, because it was an old house with squeaky floors; we couldn't flush the toilets; cell phones had to be completely off, and any other gadgets that beeped, hummed, or vibrated were banned.

When the weather was nice, we went outdoors to bask in the warmth of the sun, or killed time playing Frisbee or catch. This was fun, but not great when you were already in full hair and makeup. When it was snowing and twenty degrees out, we were cooped up in that makeup room telling jokes or watching Funny or Die videos on the computer.

There was no shortage of men in our cast who found the hair and makeup room the perfect venue to display their comedic talent. There was Danny Cosgrove, our resident funny man and wannabe rap star; and Michael O'Leary, who regularly performed his spot-on impersonations of cast and crew. Michael could do a perfect Jordan Clarke, with his garbled way of speaking, a pretty good Reva crying all the time, and a very funny Robert Newman using his hand gestures, just to name a few.

There was also Rob Bogue, who played A. C. Mallet, who over time grew incredibly fond of the prop doll we used during rehearsal for our scenes with babies. Rob regularly dressed the doll up, stuck a cigarette in its mouth, and used it as his character's bad-boy alter ego. Oh, how I miss all of those hilarious hours we spent in that room together. The sound of all of that laughter still echoes in my brain to this day.

Although some things never change about producing a soap opera, the overall dynamic of every studio we were in was unique to its environment. Three studios housed *Guiding Light* over the years. When I started in 1983, the studio was located in New York City on West Twenty-sixth Street. We then moved to East Forty-fourth Street (where Rachael Ray now shoots). The last studio we worked in was in the CBS Building on West Fifty-seventh Street, which is where we stayed from 2004 until the show ended in 2009.

Each move we made meant getting used to a new crew, because different studios are affiliated with different unions. The most difficult adjustment came in 2004, when we moved to West Fifty-seventh Street, because we had to say good-bye to a crew whom we'd been with for many years, who had become like family! Some crew members took pay cuts to make the move with us, but others just couldn't afford to change unions and lose their accrued benefits. So the show now had a studio crew who hadn't worked on a soap opera since *As the World Turns* back in 2000.

I'm not knocking the crew, but these guys weren't accustomed to working as hard as crews usually do on soap operas. They were used to crewing news programs, and let's just say they're a much easier gig! In the beginning, we would occasionally hear snoring coming from the light grids above us and find union guys sleeping behind sets! Sure, it's a long day for all of us, but excuse me. Are we keeping you up? I'm just sayin'!

It took about a month of tough love before we all got to know and admire one another. But when we did, the new crew became another wonderful new family! There is always mutual respect between actors and the crew, because without those hardworking people behind the scenes, there wouldn't be much to look at on the screen! It is a very special bond!

Every studio we worked in had a life of its own. I often referred to the elevator at the CBS studio as our "famous" elevator, because we shared studio space with BET (Black Entertainment Television). They were in one studio and we were across the hall in another. Their dressing rooms were on the same floor as ours, so it became something of a running joke that every time I wanted to get down to the set, I'd get hung up waiting for the elevator while their guests were ushered to the studio. Sometimes I'd be allowed to go along for the ride, usually with some rapper whom, of course, I didn't know. On several occasions, they'd recognize me and tell me how they used to watch our show with their grandmothers. I was always flattered and a little surprised they knew who I was. I'd have to ask someone from the crew later whom I'd been talking to! I did recognize Snoop Dogg, though, when he passed me in the hallway one day and said, "Hey, boo!" Whenever I went home and told my kids whom I saw that day, they always freaked out!

The most memorable celebrity encounter I had in that studio happened in the elevator. I had just stepped on when a large bodyguard reached in to hold the door open. I politely mentioned that I was running late and needed to get to the set. I promised to send the elevator right back up if he'd let me quickly take the ride to the floor below.

"No." That was all he said.

I think he could see that I was a little put out. I *wanted* to say, *Do you have any idea who I am?* but I didn't because he was *big*!

"Hold your horses. Relax. They're coming right now," he said, as if that were going to somehow comfort me.

I have to admit that I was pissed—especially when I saw the entourage that was headed our way. There must have been ten or twelve people trying to get on the little elevator. I didn't make any eye contact at first, but then I recognized the man in the middle of the crowd. It was none other than Stevie Wonder.

Okay, let me be frank. I am a *huge* Stevie Wonder fan. He was the first concert I ever saw live as a girl growing up in Michigan. So I was thrilled!

"Oh, my God, Stevie. You will never guess who is on the elevator with us!" I heard a woman say. It was Stevie's wife. "It's Reva Shayne! Reva Shayne is right here, standing in front of you, darling."

Well, as I'm sure you can imagine, my heart was in my throat as he extended his hand to shake mine and say hello.

"You have been my wife's constant joy in life," he said.

The only thing I could think of saying in return was "No, I believe you have that honor."

"No, ma'am. My whole house shuts down from three to four every weekday so she can watch you on *Guiding Light*. She is your biggest fan. In fact, I've watched you over the years, too!"

I had to smile, because I knew he was being so kind and—my goodness—charming. I will never forget that encounter and the many others I had over the years with actors, athletes, and musicians, including Charles Barkley, Michael Jordan, and the Rock. It turns out these guys are big fans of daytime television! I guess because they're free during the afternoons and have time to kill in their hotel room before they head to the ball field, arena, or movie set.

Most of the celebrities I've met have been through various charity events all over the country, and some have become good friends. My favorite fund-raising event is the Duke Children's Hospital celebrity golf outing held every year in Durham, North Carolina. I always make the time to tour the children's ward at the hospital, because it puts everything into perspective for me. Those kids are what the weekend is all about. I've played in that tournament about thirteen times in the past twenty years. During one particular tournament, I was approached by two beautiful teenage girls who showed me a photograph of me with them at the hospital a few days after they were born prematurely with many complications! They weren't expected to live, but through the miracle of modern medicine, there they stood in front of me as these vivacious, bright, charming young girls. They came to thank me for my participation in the tournament that raised money every year that helped save their lives! Even the clever writers from *Guiding Light* couldn't write a story like that! Of course I hugged them and wept with both girls until it was time to hit the links! What a blessing to meet them and to be reminded of how precious life truly is for all of us.

I have two beautiful elderly twins who always wait for me on the twelfth hole with a slice of homemade cake every year. There was also a family who stretched a huge banner across their yard on the sixth hole that read, ZIMMER'S TEQUILA STOP! They set up chairs and watched as all of the celebrities playing in the tournament passed by. One year I noticed these people were having a fabulous lawn party. Since it was very hot, I was particularly parched that day, so I wandered over to their party and asked if they had a beer they could spare. When the party guests realized it was me, they all flipped out. I posed for pictures and signed autographs before heading back out to the course to finish my round. As I was saying my good-byes, the hosts handed me a small cooler full of beer for my playing mates and me, on one condition—I had to do a shot of tequila with them! It was an offer I couldn't refuse. A girl's got to do what a girl's got to do, right? I looked forward to that sixth hole every year!

Back in the day I was one of very few celebrity women golfers, so I was in great demand at these tournaments. I've been fortunate enough to play rounds of golf with Yogi Berra, Spanky McFarland, Neil Armstrong, Ed Marinaro, Vince Gill, Jeff Foxworthy, Jerry Rice, Gale Sayers, Lawrence Taylor, Perry Como, Kathryn Crosby, and my two favorite buddies, Charles Barkley and number twenty-three himself, Michael Jordan. Michael and I twice cohosted a tournament to benefit the Ronald McDonald Houses of Eastern North Carolina. I'm proud to have watched him grow up from a shy young man on his first pro contract to a well-spoken, generous, and kind megastar. I haven't played a round of golf with him in ages, but if you're reading this, Michael, give me a call!

CHAPTER TEN

How I Died Three Times and Lived to Tell About It!

Soap operas are well-known for their incredible and far-fetched stories of switched paternity tests, evil twins, rampant amnesia, stolen embryos, split personalities, passionate lovers kept apart by parents, children, rivals, exes, or demonic possession, and frequent miraculous recoveries from terminal illness—or better yet, coming back from the dead. Only in the wonderful world of daytime television can a star be killed off the show, only to be resurrected and brought back for ratings, or just to make the fans happy.

As for Reva, well, she was presumed dead three different times and miraculously lived to tell all about it.

The first time Reva "died" was when I decided to leave the show in 1990. The background to the story was that when I got pregnant in real life, the writers decided to make Reva pregnant too. After Reva gave birth to her baby boy, Shayne, she began suffering from awful postpartum depression. Things got so bad that she started to have fantasies about killing herself, and also imagined that she was being chased by a phantom black van. Although Josh did his best to convince her that this was all happening in her mind, and sent her to several doctors for her depression, Reva could not be comforted.

He was finally able to convince her to get away for a few days. He thought a rest would do her good. So they took their baby boy and their daughter, Marah, and headed to Florida. They had a wonderful time until Reva got hit with one of her "red" waves.

It had been established that whenever Reva dressed in red and put on red lipstick, something bad was going to happen. Now the audience helplessly watched as Reva put on her red clothes and slowly applied her last application of red lipstick. The buildup was truly dramatic. The audience knew *something* bad was about to happen, but I don't think they knew exactly what. Sure enough, she got into her car and drove like a bat out of hell to meet Josh, where he stood on the other side of a bridge. But the bridge didn't reach across the water. It just ended halfway.

Josh was on the opposite bank waiting for Reva to arrive and witnessed her plunge into the murky water of the Florida Keys. Her last words as the car flew off the unfinished bridge were, "I'm coming, Bud!" Although he quickly dove into the water to try to save her, her body had already washed away. Neither he nor the coast guard was able to find her body, so she was presumed dead.

Viewers were left wondering whether she meant to drive off the bridge and commit suicide or if she sincerely didn't know what was about to happen. Why did she drive right through the barricades, and why didn't she hit the brakes before her car plunged into the water? Personally, I don't believe she was in her right mind when she drove off the bridge. She was suffering from such severe postpartum depression that I don't think she was even aware it was happening. But the writers intentionally left viewers wondering—and, of course, left the door cracked open for Reva to someday come back to the show.

When that happened five years later, it was revealed that Reva's body had been found by a boatload of Cuban fishermen who took her to the shore of a fictional island named San Cristobel, where they left her. The ruler of the island, Prince Richard, found Reva, but she had amnesia. She had no idea who she was or where she was from, nor any recollection of her past. Reva married the prince and became Princess Catherine of San Cristobel.

I'm just sayin'!

Reva's dramatic second death came when Annie, played by the wonderful Cynthia Watros, lured her onto an airplane whose pilot Annie killed. She then tied Reva up and left her to die as she parachuted out of the plane. The plane crashed into the Atlantic Ocean, taking Reva to a watery death . . . except she miraculously floated to the shores of another deserted island on a piece of airplane wing. There, naturally, she met the mysterious Sean McCullough, a hunky island man hiding from the law, who helped nurse her wounds. Once she had fully recuperated, she wanted to get back to Springfield. Sean, however, wanted her to remain on the island and live happily ever after with him. As sexy and tempting as he was, Reva needed to get back to Springfield to make sure Annie wasn't doing anything to hurt her children or Josh. She tried to escape the island on a homemade raft, but it sank, and struggling to survive in the rough seas, she was stung by a Portuguese man-of-war. Fortunately, Sean once again found her body washed up on shore and saved her. When she was well enough to travel, Sean revealed that he had a boat that could get her back to the mainland and agreed to take her home.

The character of Annie wasn't supposed to be a psycho until

KIM ZIMMER

I asked to come back to the show, and the producers realized that the viewing audience would want Josh and Reva to get back together. Their solution was to make Annie crazy. They spun her out of control, which made for some really compelling story lines.

Once again, Reva was back from the dead. And she had a big surprise waiting for her.

When Josh thought Reva was dead, he simply couldn't bear the thought of living without her for the rest of his life. In his grief, he allowed Dr. Michael Burke, who had successfully cloned a cat, to produce a clone of Reva with Reva's frozen eggs. The clone was born on March 6, 1998, and quickly aged with the help of an accelerated aging serum (Josh obviously wanted his adult Reva back, not a child). This was the start of one of the most controversial and unexpected story lines during *Guiding Light*.

Many fans *hated* the story on the cloning of a human being. Whenever I felt I wasn't the Reva fans wanted me to be, I would fight to maintain the integrity of the character. For example, I didn't believe Josh and Cassie should have been together as a couple, and I let everyone know how I felt. I also had moments when the writers wanted Reva to commit suicide and I didn't think it was right for her. (Of course, I ended up winning an Emmy that year based on the aftermath of her suicide attempt, so I have to concede that I wasn't always right!) Sometimes I won the battles and other times I did what I had to do, because it was my job to find ways to play a scene and keep it real—even if I thought it was ridiculous or I knew how stupid my character looked. The only thing that changed over the years that fans can blame on me without hesitation or doubt is the forty pounds I gained during my last few years on the air. Everything else was handed to me with my marching orders. Hut, two, three, four! Send in the clone! But truthfully, when it came to the clone story line, I didn't fight it because I was creatively intrigued.

Once she arrived in Springfield, Reva called home, and the voice on the other end of the line was a strangely familiar female voice. She quickly realized that something very unsettling was going on. Shortly after, Reva came face-to-face with her double, leaving her shocked and confused.

The clone took Reva captive and locked her up in the local lighthouse. Reva did whatever she could to survive and was eventually able to talk her clone into allowing her to "teach" the clone how to love Josh. The clone eventually moved Reva from the lighthouse to the pool house at the Lewis home. Reva didn't want to die in the pool house, and she knew she had to do something before it was too late; Josh was getting ready to marry the clone, even though she hadn't turned out to be the Reva of his dreams. Reva talked the clone into bringing her a camcorder so that she could watch videotapes of her children. When the clone wasn't looking, Reva was able to videotape herself so Josh would know that she was alive and being held captive in the pool house. She conned the clone into watching the tape with Josh and the kids, saying they were old family movies that would help them bond.

The clone returned to the house and popped in the tape, stopping it just in time when she realized what Reva had done. Josh overheard a part of the tape, but it didn't really hit him what he was hearing. The clone was so angry at what Reva had tried to do that she left her to starve to death in the pool house.

In the car on the way to Josh's family cabin, the clone started to feel guilty and began to ask questions about starvation. That was when Josh began to put the pieces together. He turned the car around and sped home to save his dying wife. Reunited with the real Reva, he was puzzled over what to do with the clone.

Over time, Reva had unexpectedly bonded with her clone, mostly out of pity. She decided to make the clone over into her long-lost cousin and named her Dolly, after the first real-life cloned sheep. (In a running gag, every time I walked on the set as Dolly, the crew would all *baaaa* like sheep!) Dolly began to settle into her new identity, but Reva still had a lot of unresolved anger with Josh for cloning her, and for giving up on their love.

Dolly, who was still very much in love with Josh, decided her new life wasn't what she wanted. She took an overdose of aging serum so that she would die, and Josh and Reva would be able to move on with their life together.

Five months after she was born, Dolly committed suicide on August 10, 1998, at the age of one hundred thirty-four, in the arms of the original Reva.

In an interview with *Daytime Confidential*, our former executive producer Paul Rauch came clean about who was behind the controversial cloning story line. "We did a lot of different stories on [*One Life to Live*], like Viki goes to heaven, and Clint goes back in time and Eterna, which . . . were No. 1 rated stories during sweeps period. However, *Guiding Light* is not the kind of show that should be doing stories like that. But the network and [Procter & Gamble] came to me one day and said, 'We think this is a story you should do.' And there was just no saying no. When they got tired of the story, the network said, 'Give

Reva a drink that ages her so she'll die and we can get out of this.' I always believed that story belonged on a show like [*One Life to Live*] or *Days*. It doesn't belong on *Guiding Light* because it's a show about family and social interaction."

As absurd as the clone story was, I personally liked it because it stimulated me as an actress. I got to play two characters with a lot of similarities (Dolly was, after all, a clone!) but subtle differences.

Confusing, right?

Try playing those two women!

My dialogue practically doubled, which meant I had more lines to learn in the same amount of time. It was incredibly daunting to memorize, on average, seventy pages of dialogue a day, on top of the extra-long shooting days demanded because the scenes that the clone and Reva were in together had to be shot twice. My cast mates moaned and groaned when they had scenes with Reva and Dolly, because they had to shoot everything twice too, as well as wait around for my costume and makeup changes. Still, I have to admit that creatively it was a very interesting challenge for me—not to mention the bump in salary I got for playing two parts.

My third and final death came in 2006, when Reva developed breast cancer.

Breast cancer wasn't a new story line to our show. In fact, in 1980 Nurse Lillian Raines, played by Tina Sloan, was the first character in daytime to battle breast cancer. Her story was inspired by Kathy Chambers, one of the show's producers, who had died from breast cancer before I was part of the cast.

I was excited about the prospect of playing a part that would raise awareness about the disease, and it was important that I play it in an authentic way. There's a lot of pressure playing a story that you know so many women are going to connect to. I had never been through a breast cancer scare, but my sister had it (I am happy to say she has been cancer-free for many years), so I knew what it was like from the perspective of a loved one. But I didn't know what it would be like to actually go through it. I was reluctant to do a lot of research, because I wanted Reva to experience it fresh and real. I did read *Breast Cancer for Dummies* from the series of yellow paperbacks that gives you the basics on every imaginable subject, and several other books on dealing with breast cancer. Those books were very helpful to me as an actress, because they didn't go into a lot of specifics. They gave me clear guidelines to live between. I also spent some time talking to people I knew who had gone through breast cancer. I had each of them tell me about their experiences, and interestingly, they were all completely different. I was surer than ever that I should approach Reva's battle with breast cancer in a spontaneous, organic way.

Reva's breast cancer story became very controversial—not because of her cancer, per se, but because she chose not to tell anyone she cared about what she was going through, especially Josh. Fans of the show were livid with her decision, because Josh was her soul mate, the love of her life. He'd surely have wanted to know if she was sick. Thousands of letters came in asking why she wouldn't share such an important part of her life with him.

It turned out that the writers had gotten the idea from a true story they had read in the newspaper about a woman who had chosen to go through chemotherapy without telling anyone in her family. She hid her hair loss by wearing wigs; she told family members she wanted to change her look, so she was experimenting with different styles. She was able to get through her treatments without anyone knowing until she was well on the road to recovery.

While many people saw Reva's decision to keep her illness from Josh as selfish, it was not. In fact, for the first time in her life, Reva was being selfless, not selfish. She wanted Josh to have his own life. He was now in a relationship with Reva's sister. She didn't want her illness to come between them. She'd drop hints from time to time, but whenever Josh was getting too close, Reva shut him down, because she didn't want him to change his life plan for her, especially if she wasn't going to make it.

While Reva lay in her hospital bed, bald and frail from battling her cancer, I was battling behind the scenes over some contract issues that no one was certain would be worked out. The suits were convinced we wouldn't come to an agreement, so they gave themselves the opportunity to "kill" Reva for the third time.

Reva flatlined on a Friday, leaving viewers believing she was dead. But Monday she was awake, and by Tuesday she was walking out of the hospital.

It was nothing short of a miracle.

Not that Reva lived—that we worked out the details of my contract so I wouldn't leave the show!

Look, I am aware that lots of the stories we did over the years were far-fetched, if not a little absurd, but that's what soap operas are all about. They really are for the "Calgon, take me away" moments we all need. Viewers tune in to escape the problems and drama of their own lives, and maybe a little bit to feel like their lives are okay compared to the tormented fictional lives of the characters!

For an hour viewers get to sit down and live vicariously through these characters and their passionate love lives, get a glimpse of some stylish clothes, jewelry, and homes, and fantasize what it would be like to be "us." It's a safe escape from their world into ours. Everyone loves to daydream from time to time. In fact, we had a character on *Guiding Light* who often had dreams that she was a Broadway dancer, or living in *Casablanca*. Fans loved her because she had these elaborate fantasies that the viewer could relate to.

The bottom line is, you can't please everybody. When soaps got away from the out-of-the-realm-of-possibility story lines and began doing more realistic stories about abortion, cancer, and other heavy topics, they sometimes hit a little too close to home for some fans, who complained that the fantasy was gone. But if these stories are well written and told three-dimensionally, which many were, it's possible to strike gold; the fans end up embracing the story as lived by their favorite character. I know that when Reva suffered through her breast cancer, I received many letters from women with breast cancer who found the story difficult to watch yet also loved it, because it gave them hope for survival. I embraced these letters; they kept me motivated to make sure we were telling the story as truthfully as possible.

Reva not only died three times, but she also attempted suicide. Her heart was broken in 1985, when Kyle Sampson, the first true love Reva had since Josh had left town, had an affair with his ex-lover Maeve Stoddard. Maeve was a very wealthy newspaperwoman who came back to Springfield to reconnect with Kyle. When Reva discovered his infidelity, she was devastated. She had already lost the original love of her life, Josh, and now she was losing Kyle, whom she'd really given her heart to! Reva became so depressed that she saw suicide as the only answer.

Oh, did I pitch a fit! I didn't believe that Reva would *ever* do such a thing. I told the writers that Reva was too selfish to commit suicide; there was no way she'd ever do it.

It was a battle I lost. So I decided that, if I had to play this out, I would really give it my all. I knew many of the fans wouldn't believe that Reva was going to commit suicide any more than I did. To overcome this dilemma, the story line had to be plausible, so I emotionally took her to the very edge— literally. As an actor, you have to remove any personal feelings you have about a decision your character is making and play it for truth and authenticity. So when it came time for me to shed my white fox fur and fall over the railing of a bridge wearing nothing but the sexiest little teddy, I did it with reckless abandon! What a way to go, right?

Of course, once Reva hit the water she realized that she wanted to live and pulled herself back from the brink! In an ironic twist, I was actually nominated for an Emmy that year for *this story line*. Go figure!

Not only that, but a lot of viewers wrote me that they had been contemplating suicide, but when they saw Reva pull herself back from the edge, they knew they could do it too. These were powerful stories that affected so many people!

Suicide is never the answer to life's problems. There is always a better solution. Life throws us all curves from time to time. It isn't those circumstances that define us so much as how we respond to them. Reva was indestructible, and I loved that about her. She faced her troubled and challenging life with a survivor mentality, taking one step at a time, embracing each day as a new opportunity to start again. And boy, oh, boy, did she know how to start again.

CHAPTER ELEVEN

Seven Husbands

When people ask me how I've managed to maintain such a successful marriage for thirty years, I always give them the same answer: *I had it made.* Along the way, I got to have affairs and live out almost every fantasy possible through the characters I've played on TV. I was flown all over the world to exotic and romantic locations, got seduced in every corner, was bathed in lemon juice before making love in an Amish farmhouse, given a sponge bubble bath surrounded by lots of candles, and received fancy jewelry and gifts. Hey, it was my job, and best of all, I got paid to do it!

As Nola on *The Doctors*, Echo on *One Life to Live*, Jody on *Santa Barbara*, and finally Reva on *Guiding Light*, I could make out with and pretend to be "in love" with some of the most beautiful men on daytime television.

During my career, I got to fall into the arms of Glenn Corbett and Alec Baldwin on *The Doctors*, Clint Ritchie on *One Life to Live*, and A Martinez on *Santa Barbara*. But I must confess that my favorite lovers were my men of *Guiding Light*! There was a reason I baptized myself "the Slut of Springfield"! My character simply could not get enough of them.

The show was packed with a full roster of dreamy men any woman would swoon over. There was Jordan Clarke (Billy Lewis), who had the softest, sweetest lips ever! Of course, he usually had just eaten a huge hamburger with a huge slice of onion on it before our kissing scenes. He wasn't eating onions to be cruel—he was a big ol' cowboy and liked onions on his burgers. It didn't really bother me, though one of his other leading ladies, Maeve Kincaid, wasn't too appreciative. In the end, what Jordan ate for lunch never mattered, because he was like a big cuddly teddy bear who was never afraid to show his emotions. Then there was Justin Deas (Buzz Cooper), who acted with such passion that kissing him was like receiving a knockout punch from Muhammad Ali! And I truly mean that as a compliment. Hey, if you're going to be knocked out, better it be by "the greatest," right?

Another favorite of mine was the wonderful Larkin Malloy as Kyle Sampson, who was the king of the "eye-lock romance." Our characters fell in love after parachuting out of a crashing plane and plummeting through the roof of an Amish farmhouse. Larkin always looked deep into my eyes before he kissed me, and it would send shock waves up and down my spine! The Reva-Kyle romance was based on fantasy from the very beginning. The whole story unfolded when a portrait of Reva showed up in Springfield as a gift to her with no note or information about whom it came from. That was the beginning of the mystery that led Reva into the arms of Kyle Sampson. Kyle was a man of mystery who swept Reva off her feet from the moment they met. Kyle and Reva had several imagined and memorable romantic fantasy encounters that never happened, and a few that did, including a bubble-bath scene that we couldn't seem to get just right. The bubbles kept popping, so the camera could see my body stocking in the shot. It was really annoying to keep starting the scene over, because it was hard to get into the moment again and again. I finally got so frustrated that I said, "Screw it," and wiggled out of the top part of my body stocking, leaving me completely topless so we could get the scene done. We were leaning into each other, face-to-face. I was bare-chested, but I trusted Larkin enough to know he wasn't going anywhere he wasn't supposed to go.

Other fantasies included Larkin playing a sea captain who captures Reva the mermaid, and a dream sequence set to Billy Ocean's "Suddenly" on a gorgeous country-club set amid fog machines! I can only imagine what fun our head writers Pamela Long and Jeff Ryder had coming up with those fantasy sequences!

Reva craved one thing in her life: romance. She was the kind of woman who made men go wild—and there were more than a few. But her great love was and will always be Joshua Lewis. Josh was played by the very special and talented man who helped me win all four of my Emmys, Robert Newman, whom by now you know I love and adore both on- and offscreen.

To many, the characters portrayed on their favorite shows are real, and there were plenty of people I met over the years who assumed that Robert Newman and I were married in real life. It wasn't unusual to go someplace and have a stranger walk up to me and ask about my husband. When I'd say he was home in New Jersey with the kids, they'd look at me with utter confusion in their eyes. At that point I knew to ask *which* husband they were referring to, and frequently it was "Josh." Even though I think most people knew we were just the actors playing Josh and Reva, they wanted to believe we were these characters to keep the fantasy alive.

The connection between the Lewises and the Shaynes dates back to Reva's childhood. For as long as she could recall, Reva wanted to be married to one of the Lewis boys—but most especially to Josh. Being his wife was her only goal in life. When she went to the Lewis family mansion and helped her mother clean their house, she secretly fantasized that one day she too would be a Lewis.

The three Lewis children, Trish, Billy, and Josh, were terrible to Reva. They poked fun at her all the time. Robert and Jordan would always laugh, thinking up ways their characters might have tortured Reva. They thought it was really funny to imagine seeing Reva on the side of the road getting splashed with muddy water as they drove through a puddle. Boys will be boys!

Reva was so full of verve and laughter, always the life of the party. She also had an insatiable need to be loved and to love. Her schoolgirl crush on Josh eventually led to a relationship that was pure, raw, honest, and real. It was the type of love that could come only from the soul. It ran so deep that it was impenetrable. It was a love no one else could touch. It took passion to a higher level. And when they made love, it was more than just sex. It was lovemaking in every way. There would never be another man who would affect Reva or capture her heart like Joshua.

So how come Reva married Josh's brother, Billy? When Josh left to go to college, she felt utterly abandoned. The separation was more than she could stand, so she married Billy to get back at him for leaving her. She knew that her hooking up with someone else wouldn't have the same impact on Josh as losing the great love of his life to his only brother. Billy was a wild stallion and better by far in bed. He and Reva made mad, passionate, wild love. Their relationship was all about the sex. Reva became pregnant, but she hid it from everyone except her mother, Sarah, who sent her away to have the baby she would ultimately give up for adoption.

Through her relationship with Josh and Billy, Reva grew close to their father, H. B. Lewis, played by the wonderful Larry Gates. Anytime you had a scene with Larry, it was gold. In my mind, H. B. Lewis, the patriarch of the Lewis family, was the best man Reva ever had in her life. He understood the complexities of her character, and because of his warmth and compassion, she, in turn, had the utmost respect for him.

H.B. was the father figure Reva had never had. She could always go to him when she felt hurt, slighted, or disappointed by one of his sons. H.B. offered Reva his unconditional love, something Reva had never known in her life. They got along famously, sharing the same interests and savoring the best life had to offer. He opened doors for Reva no one else could or would, which in her mind gave her the opportunity to become "someone."

Robert Newman and I always agreed that the romantic triangle of H.B., Josh, and Reva was our *Cat on a Hot Tin Roof* story line. We always thought of Larry Gates as Big Daddy, Josh as Brick, and me as Maggie the Cat. I think it kind of embarrassed Larry on some level after Reva and H.B. became romantically involved. He never saw himself as a romantic leading man, but because of Larry's sensitive portrayal of the character, the audience believed everything H.B. did. Whenever Larry and I had to be romantic with each other, we'd laugh, but when the cameras rolled, we were two people terribly in love!

One of my all-time favorite moments on the show took place after H.B. and Reva decided to unexpectedly elope to Hawaii. When they returned a married couple, the family totally disapproved. In fact, Josh went as far as to call his father an old man and told him that he would never be able to satisfy a woman like Reva Shayne. The writers crafted a beautiful scene where Reva came to H.B.'s bed (they always had separate bedrooms) and asked him to make love to her. In that tender moment, she confessed that she loved him and wanted their marriage to be complete. I will never forget the way Larry portrayed H.B. in those scenes. His deep vulnerability broke my heart. He made it so easy to love H.B.

When Reva became pregnant with H.B.'s baby, she was overjoyed at the prospect of their bringing a child into the world together. However, when Josh heard the news, he left Springfield for the Lewis oil fields of Venezuela, where he met and married a beautiful woman named Sonni. Shortly after Josh left, Reva was hit by a car driven by the drugged Vanessa Reardon and suffered a miscarriage, which broke her heart and H.B.'s too. The loss was so devastating that it led to the ultimate demise of their relationship. At the end of the season, Larry Gates was nominated for an Emmy award for his work on that story line. His win was well deserved!

Reva's next husband was Alan Spaulding, played by the fantastic and talented Mr. Ron Raines. The cast made sure to call him "Mr. Ron Raines," because something about him seemed to command respect. Honestly, I don't think I've ever met anyone in my life quite like Ron. For starters, it's almost impossible to say anything bad about him, because he's one of the nicest men in the business. He worked very hard to be the ideal Alan Spaulding, because he was so kind in real life that he found it very difficult be such a villainous character. When we were working together quite a bit, he always made sure a hot cappuccino was waiting for me in my dressing room whenever we had scenes together first thing in the morning. I think it was Ron's way of making sure I would behave and not try to screw with him in our scenes together. Although I rarely tried to trip up a fellow actor, there *were* times I found it irresistible to play practical jokes on someone—especially Ron! He was such an easy target, because he was so focused on work and his character that he never saw it coming. I would ad-lib a line to try to throw him and have fun watching him figure out how to respond to whatever I had just said while staying in character. I have to admit he was always a good sport about those moments. I enjoyed it because there was nothing better than seeing Ron laugh.

Ron was hilarious, especially when he forgot his lines. He'd start ad-libbing bizarre dialogue and keep going until someone in the control booth was able to stop laughing long enough to yell, "Cut!"

Ron's character, Alan, who had formerly been played by Chris Bernau, was responsible for bringing Reva to Springfield, of course, where she quickly became a pain in everyone's ass! To help with her assignment to break up Billy's engagement, Alan had set Reva up to look like a wealthy woman, with fancy fur coats, jewelry, and lots of champagne. Later, she'd lived the high life and had all of the material things she so desperately wanted while married to H.B. So she was easily seduced by Alan's money and power. Alan married Reva while she was in a coma suffered from saving Josh's life after his Jeep went off the road and plunged into the icy river. I don't really know how this could have happened; after all, I was in a *coma*. I'm sure there are laws against this type of marriage, but hey, that's daytime! When Reva awoke, she realized that although she cared a great deal for Alan, in her heart she knew he didn't love her so much as he wanted to possess her.

One of the hardest things I ever had to do on *Guiding Light* was a scene where I had to slap Alan. I certainly didn't mind slapping Alan Spaulding, but I hated slapping Ron. I've hit a lot of men on daytime, but I was never as nervous as I was in the scene with Ron.

I worried that he would get angry if I slapped him the wrong way. And what if I ended up hurting him?

My nerves got the best of me, because when it came time, I ended up missing the fatty part of his cheek and clocking him right in the ear—which might be the most painful place you can slap someone. Let me tell you, Ron got a whole lot of mileage out of my mistake after that day of shooting. The snarky comments lasted for weeks, maybe even months. Whenever I tried to poke fun at him, he pulled out his trump card: "I'm sorry. I didn't hear you because of the ringing in my ears from when you injured me!"

Ron is a true gentleman. He is the guy who never forgets a birthday, and always gets a kick out of finding the perfect card. Sometimes he brought people five cards, each funnier than the last. Even though the birthday greetings were often terribly mean-spirited, everyone had to admit that they were still ridiculously funny. I really loved working with Ron.

After Reva's divorce from Alan, and much to the delight of the fans, Josh and Reva finally got married in 1989. The ceremony took place at Cross Creek, the Lewis family estate in Oklahoma, and the spot where they had made love for the first time as teenagers. When they exchanged their vows, one of the most memorable scenes in all my years on the show, Josh said to Reva, "From this moment on, we are going to be the family that we were always meant to be. The family that we always were. Always, Reva."

Then Reva uttered two words that became the emblem of their relationship: "Always, Bud."

Josh and Reva were married for about a year before she drove her car off the ill-fated bridge in Florida and was presumed dead. And even though Josh spent years searching for her, it was Alan Spaulding who found her very much alive and living in Goshen, Pennsylvania, on an Amish farm as "Rebecca." It was never revealed how Reva went from being Catherine, the princess of San Cristobel, to Rebecca of the Amish farm. I used to laugh, conjuring images of Princess Catherine wearing a ball gown and tiara, somehow hitchhiking from San Cristobel to Goshen to end up as an Amish healer. This transition baffled even me.

She had no recollection of her life as Reva, until one day her memory returned when Alan mentioned Springfield. Alan wanted Reva for himself and did everything he could to prevent her from returning to Springfield and the arms of her one true love. Alas, when she did get home, her one true love was not waiting for her. He had finally accepted her death and had moved on with his life; he was now in love with a nurse named Annie Dutton.

Josh and Reva came face-to-face on the night of Josh and Annie's wedding. Of course, it's a soap opera, so it became clear to everyone in their lives that Josh and Reva were far from over. Still, Josh was committed to Annie, who was now acting as mother to Reva's children, Marah and Shayne. Since Reva had been gone for five years, they thought of Annie as their mother.

Reva was passionate about the men in her life, but she was truly in love with her two children. She ceded the kids to Annie out of her intense desire to give them a stable family environment—something she doubted she could give them. Out of frustration and grieving the loss, Reva married Buzz Cooper. Buzz described Reva as the only woman on earth who made his life "heaven and hell." Buzz was a good man who gave Reva a much-needed break; he didn't judge her, he gave her space, and he saved her life, because their relationship came at a time when Reva was dealing with the terrible loss of Josh. Buzz swept her up and gave her a very simple life—something she desperately needed. She grew to love him with all her heart because he put up with her (and, of course, they also enjoyed a very healthy sex life!). Buzz opened Reva's eyes to a different type of power from what Alan or H.B. had had in the past: the power of family and love and devotion to a cause. He was a wonderful replacement for Josh, but deep down, I think she understood that her relationship with Buzz wasn't meant to last. Reva simply couldn't stay away from Josh.

As if my cup hadn't already run over with handsome men, I also got to be in love with Bradley Cole as two different characters! First, he played Prince Richard Winslow, who fell in love with Reva when she washed up on the shore of his island after driving her car off the bridge.

Richard was very proper. Bradley played him with that royal stiffness that you'd expect. Our love was rich in propriety. The writers eventually killed Richard off, but because of popular demand, Bradley came back to the show in 2003 as the randy playboy (and Reva's seventh husband) Jeffrey O'Neill.

Bradley was a bad boy, just like his character. Even though Jeffrey allegedly bedded just about every woman in Springfield, it was the irrepressible, irresistible Reva Shayne who was able to get him to the altar. Bradley, as Jeffrey, was so much fun to have love scenes with. Of course, there was still nervous laughter, but Bradley and I incorporated that sense of fun into our on-screen relationship. As the relationship progressed, Bradley's kisses became more playful as well. There was no longer tension in his lips. His kisses became comfortable and enjoyable. I know he's going to kill me for saying that.

Toward the end of *Guiding Light*'s run, the writers decided they wanted Reva to have one more child. In typical daytime fashion, no one cared that this pregnancy was coming after Reva had already gone through menopause. While the chances of getting pregnant postmenopause are nil—it is not medically possible to conceive if you have stopped ovulating—through the miracle of television and tremendously creative writing, Reva became pregnant by Jeffrey O'Neill during her battle with breast cancer. The cancer medication she was taking was also a fertility drug, so despite the obvious, she was able to get pregnant. The doctors recommended she abort the baby, because they needed to treat her cancer with extreme measures and radiation. That was a nonstarter; Reva loved children too much to lose one by choice, so instead, she waited to get treatment until she safely gave birth. She saw this baby as a miracle for her and Jeffrey, because neither one of them had been there for their children's lives.

I have to admit that I loved having a baby bump again, because it had been nineteen years since I had had my last kid. It was really fun to put the pad on and have someplace to rest my arms. All those things you do when you are really pregnant come back to you like it was yesterday. For example, I used to rub my belly all the time, and when I watched those episodes, I noticed Reva doing the same thing. I wasn't even aware I was doing it when we were filming! It was just bizarre, because, of course, I wasn't really pregnant. Still, it was really fun to feel that way again after so many years.

The Reva-Jeffrey relationship had a real freshness to it. The writers dubbed their story line a "what the hell!" relationship, because it was never meant to be more than a diversion for Reva while Josh was having a fling with Reva's sister, Cassie. Much to the writers' surprise, our audience loved the flirtation between the two characters, so the writers decided to take the relationship to the next level—a relationship with "no strings attached"!

Since we were both older and had been through so many things in our lives, all of our decisions were pretty much the same and driven by our "what the hell" attitude.

"What the hell—let's be more than just friends."

"What the hell—let's live together."

"What the hell—let's have a baby."

"What the hell—let's get married."

And then one day, Jeffrey just disappeared. He left to hunt down the man who had been making threats to his family. He knew he had to kill this man or Jeff, Reva, and their newborn baby, Colin, would never be safe. So there she was with a newborn, an absent husband, and breast cancer. Only Reva!

Despite his bad-boy image on-screen, Bradley was a terrific and caring man. And it was thanks to him that I had had the opportunity every year to pretend I was a rock star. He routinely put together special evenings of entertainment to benefit the American Red Cross, a cause that was very near and dear to his heart. He and his band would play backup for about ten different performers from various soaps, and whatever proceeds they collected at the end of the night were donated to the American Red Cross. My favorite songs to sing at these events were "I'm the Only One" by Melissa Etheridge, "Proud Mary," and "Queen Bee" from the movie *A Star Is Born*—and any other folky rock songs that came to mind. The fund-raisers were always a success, and the actors who took part had a great time. I always enjoyed supporting my fellow actors in championing their worthy causes. We are all so blessed to have the opportunities our careers have allowed us, and we are grateful for those blessings every single day.

Being with all of these men was wonderful. Each of them was sexy, fun, and so very handsome. Mark Dobies, who played Noah Chase, was a fantastic kisser! We developed a wonderful friendship and spent a lot of downtime together talking about our kids, spouses, and careers. One of the greatest things about Mark was that he was also a personal trainer with a rock-solid physique. We're talking zero percent body fat! He made me work out with him every morning for an hour, which was a godsend, because left to my own devices I'd much rather have been in the makeup room gossiping with the rest of the cast than running my ass off in a gym.

I can't really say who the best kisser of the bunch was, because they all had their own individual style. But I can tell you there was one actor I auditioned with many years ago who still holds the title of worst kisser. He shoved his tongue down my throat, which is considered an absolute professional no-no. I can't recall any other actor attempting to do that over the years.

Love scenes on television may look sexy and feel romantic when you're watching, but the truth is, doing them is really not all that it is cracked up to be. I'm sure you won't believe me, but I have to break the news to you: Love scenes on soaps are the most unromantic, uncomfortable, and mechanical thing that actors contend with on a set. It is one hundred percent true! There are actors and directors who are better at it than others, but it is never a pleasurable experience for anyone involved. Every movement has to be carefully planned. Put your hand here, kiss her neck here, slide your hand down his back here, and clench your fist at the moment of ecstasy here. A good director will pull it all together so that it looks natural and spontaneous, when it is anything but.

On *Guiding Light*, we had on average four or five contract directors, and they all had their own unique way of shooting love scenes. In my opinion, the two most talented love scene directors happened to be women. My favorite director was a woman named JoAnne Sedwick. Joanne always set the most romantic scene for the audience and had a terrific eye for romance. Irene Pace was also very good with love scenes. Both women would be very clear to let us know their plan with the camera. They'd give us a lot of specifics, such as, "The camera is going to pan up her bare leg, so run your hand up her leg and stop at her bottom, and leave your hand there, palm open."

Unlike the female directors, the male directors liked it *rough*! Our longtime senior director and my good friend Bruce Barry shot love scenes as if he were working for the Playboy Channel! They were always extremely hot but also a wee bit nasty as well. One scene had an actress on our show being mounted from behind. I have no idea how that got past Standards and Practices— you know, the folks who sit around and decide what is or is not allowed to air. They would monitor everything, from how much skin was shown in love scenes to the number of cuss words in the scripts; we had a weekly quota, and once you were over the limit, that was it until the next week. Damn! To this day, Bruce still denies it was anything other than beautifully romantic and tasteful. But I often thought that if my daytime gig didn't end up working out, after working with Bruce, I could always turn to porn! Don't worry. I still love ya, Brucester!

Pulling off a love scene on camera boils down to trust. It's up to the actors to decide how far they can each go. Love scenes are actually easier to do when you don't know your partner very well. The reason is simple: There's less acting involved because, well, the relationship is new. There's some authentic chemistry in a new relationship. When you have to play love scenes with someone you know well, it's like playing a love scene with your brother! Direction is incredibly important in these scenes, because "the giggle factor" kicks in if two actors are left to their own devices. That's exactly what happened with Mark and me when we did our first love scene together. We giggled through the whole thing, because I think we were both so embarrassed. That relationship could have been so much better if there had been more sensuality between us. But maybe it didn't matter; we both knew our on-screen relationship wasn't going to develop into a real love affair, because Josh was already working his way back into Reva's life.

The longer Robert Newman and I worked together, the harder it was to keep a straight face during love scenes, because we'd become such good friends and knew each other's spouses so well. Sometimes in rehearsal we'd crack each other up, but when the cameras rolled the fantasy kicked in and we'd make magic together. You can't become a supercouple without great love scenes! Well, there was one exception. Tom Pelphrey and I were often called a "supercouple"—and he played my son!

The character of Jonathan Randall was conceived at a time when I had become bored with the forward progress of my character. And it appeared that the fans agreed the story had gotten boring. You need conflict in a soap, and we had none. Josh and Reva were happily married, our kids were happy, so the producers felt it was time to cue some trouble! That trouble came in the form of a bad boy with a chip on his shoulder the size of the Grand Canyon.

Jonathan Randall was born to Reva and Prince Richard while she was suffering from amnesia and living as his princess on San Cristobel. The viewing audience knew they'd had a baby together but believed that the baby had been given up for adoption. They didn't know Catherine had actually given the baby away to save his life. The evil Prince Edmund, who was Prince Richard's brother, wanted to kill the baby to retain his place in line for the throne. That was when Catherine placed the baby in the hands of her friend Olivia, to be raised by Olivia's sister and her abusive husband. Many years later, Jon showed up in Springfield on a mission to ruin the life of this woman, Reva. Our two characters shared an immense, emotional, "no-holds-barred" attitude about everything in life!

They brought in seven young men for this role and asked me to do the audition scene with each one so the producers could see whether there was chemistry between us. I was surprised that I wasn't auditioning ten-year-old boys, since it had been ten years since the baby story line. Instead, the character had been SORASed. (As you may know, "Soap Opera Rapid Aging Syndrome" is a common disorder in the world of daytime television; it causes a child character to skip numerous years of life and reappear a lot older than he or she would normally be!) So instead of ten-year-old boys, I was meeting twenty-four-year-old hotties. I thought each of the men was very handsome and a wonderful actor, except for one, a badass named Tom. As hard as I tried, I couldn't get a rise or reaction out of that kid. Not a tear or a laugh or even a smile. Not a sign of softness or vulnerability, two traits that are so important in daytime television. I thought he was just plain mean!

What I didn't know was that he'd been told by the producers to do his best to freak me out! Well, he succeeded! When the scenes were over, the suits asked me which one of the actors I liked. I said that I would be happy to work with any of them, except for Tom.

The next morning, Tom Pelphrey was my new son, Jonathan Randall! When Tom first showed up on the set, I called him

"Cub," because I thought he was just a young rookie. Boy, was I wrong about that. Thank the good Lord that no one listened to me, because my work with Tom was the most exciting and exhilarating that I had ever done with another actor. Tom tested me and my craft in ways I hadn't experienced in years. His presence on the set woke me up again. He gave me a shot in the arm that I desperately needed, even though I hadn't known it. I will be forever grateful for his gifts, talent, and presence in my life. He was my perfect foil. We were indeed a "supercouple" without ever swapping spit! I look forward to watching this incredible actor's journey, as I am sure he will continue to do great work.

There have been lots of stories about actors falling in love with their costars over the years—which I can understand, because, God knows, I could have fallen for all of my leading men if it weren't for my great and undying love for my real-life one and only man, A.C. Being married to an actress is not easy on many levels, but being married to an actress whose job is to bed every good-looking man who comes through Springfield surely had to be hard. I have to thank my loving and supportive husband for understanding that what I do is just a job. At the end of the day, I come home to his warm and strong embrace, and to me, there is and never will be anything better.

CHAPTER TWELVE

Everything's Coming Up Rosie

Every talk or variety television show has its favorite guests. These are the people the bookers like to have on their show because they know they'll always draw the largest viewing audience or get the biggest laugh. David Letterman loves to have Regis Philbin; Alec Baldwin has hosted Saturday Night Live more than any other performer; and me? Well, I've had a few memorable experiences doing talk shows too.

Rosie O'Donnell enjoyed watching *Guiding Light* from time to time, but lucky for me, she was a true fan of Kim Zimmer. She loved having me as a guest on her show, which I had done several times over the years.

Then one night I took my daughter to see a New York Liberty basketball game at Madison Square Garden. The Liberty is the New York WNBA team. We were invited to the game by our good friend Anya Barrett. I thought Rachel, who played basketball on her high school team at the time, might enjoy going to a game. When we checked in at the "will call" window to pick up our tickets that night, we were approached by an official-looking young man wearing a headset.

"How would you two like to compete in our mother-daughter competition? We are having minigames at the end of every period."

Rachel thought it would be really cool to participate. I wasn't sure whether I should tell him who I was or not. I didn't want to have it seem like we were picked because I'm an actress. Rachel gave me a look that basically said, *Keep your mouth shut!* So I didn't say a word.

The first period went by, then the second. After the first half of the game I began to wonder if we had somehow been disqualified. But then someone came over to our seats to get us so we could get ready to play during the next break. I happened to be wearing a short skirt and thong underwear that night, so I was hoping and praying there wasn't going to be a lot of bending over involved in our little game. It turns out that we were going to be a part of the mother-daughter shoot-out. They handed us two huge T-shirts to wear—personally, I was hoping for an authentic Liberty jersey, but no such luck. We were paired up against another mother-daughter team that was daunting from the start. The mother was approximately six and a half feet tall. Her daughter was "only" six foot three! Yikes. I thought we were doomed from the moment they stepped onto the court.

We were told that all we had to do was toss up a bunch of free throws. Whichever team got the most baskets in the couple of minutes we played won. Simple enough, right? They gave Rachel and me a rack of balls and told Rachel to throw first. I am proud to say she sank four shots.

Then the other daughter went. Thank God she sank only two.

All righty, then! I thought. *We might actually have a chance here!*

Except now it was my turn to throw.

I did the best I could, but standing at the free-throw line, I couldn't even get the ball to the basket! It was pathetic.

Somehow, in spite of my lame efforts, we miraculously won. Rachel was so excited that she picked me up in her arms and twirled me around. I started laughing really hard, because I was certain that my T-shirt had ridden up along with my skirt and that I was flashing my ass to everyone in the Garden!

A week later, I appeared on *The Rosie O'Donnell Show*. I confidently walked from behind the stage to her desk, where I sat down ready for a great interview—as always.

"I saw your heinie!"

Yes. Those were the first words of our interview before she broke into a little tune about my fanny: "I saw your heinie so bright and shiny!" I was mortified! We had a good laugh over the incident at the Garden. And as an added bonus, Rosie told me she thought I had a nice ass!

Two weeks later, my cast mate Ricky Paull Goldin appeared on Rosie's show and she gave him a package to deliver to me: a lovely selection of underwear! It's not as weird as it sounds, though; she had started a charity fund-raiser, Celebrity Thongs. She was asking various celebrities to send in an autographed pair of their underwear, which she auctioned off for a good cause.

Now, for many people, doing the Oprah show is a dream come true. For me, well, not so much. I appeared on Oprah's show two times. The first was for a show about daytime power couples, and Robert Newman and I were among a panel of guests. That particular show was uneventful and went off without a hitch.

The second and last time I appeared on *Oprah* was in the late eighties. This show featured Deidre Hall, Jill Larson, Marcy Walker, Robin Strasser, Jeanne Cooper, Susan Lucci, and me, representing the leading ladies of soaps from all three networks at the time. We sat in a long row of chairs onstage as Oprah began her chat. It turned out that Oprah was a huge fan of the ABC soaps, and that she was especially a fan of Susan Lucci and Marcy Walker. The entire first segment passed by without a single word directed at me, or Deidre for that matter, as Oprah asked all of her questions to Susan, Robin, Jill, and Marcy, the women from ABC. Jeanne jumped in on her own, because that is just who she is. I sat there like a bump on a log. I thought, *Oh, well, she'll get to me in the next segment.* Wrong! We came back from the commercial break and I was ready to jump in. Still, there was no question lobbed my way. At least there were a couple of "general" questions to the group that I could pounce on, yet none that were actually directed at me.

At the next commercial break, I got up, removed my mic, and decided to leave the set. I didn't want to sit there and look like an idiot, which was how I felt. I might as well have sat in the audience that day and enjoyed the show as a viewer, from the comfort of their seats. As I headed for the exit, one of the producers stopped me. It might have been Gayle King; who can remember . . . ?

"Where are you going?" she asked.

"I have to leave because I'm not a part of the conversation." I was not a happy camper.

"No, no, no! You can't leave!" The producer was pleading with me, but it was too late. I was too embarrassed. I was embarrassed for myself, for my mom who would be watching at home, and for all of the fans of *Guiding Light* who would surely be disappointed that Oprah clearly wasn't a fan.

I made my way backstage and began walking down the long hallway leading toward my dressing room. I was in a huff and wanted to speak to my publicist, who had accompanied me to the show.

"I'd like to leave." That was all I said when I finally found her. Before she could utter a comforting word, I heard the *click, click, click* of Oprah's high heels on the tiled floor coming from behind me. My heart was pounding so hard. I didn't want to have a confrontation with Oprah—I just wanted to get out of there.

"Kim, I want to explain this to you." She began to speak in the humblest and most apologetic tone. "I am a fan of *All My Children* and I got a little carried away and I am sorry. But you've taught me a huge lesson. I cannot apologize to you enough. Please come back and finish the show."

In that moment, I realized why Oprah is who she is! She was honest, candid, and real. She apologized, and owned her mistake. My ego had gotten the best of me, but it was Oprah's lack of ego that allowed her to address the problem head-on and deal with it before anything could spiral out of control.

I agreed to return to the studio on one condition: She had to ask me one question. Just one. She laughed and said she had lots of notes on me and would be happy to ask me as many questions as she possibly could in the time we had left.

I also learned an important lesson that day. I realized that sometimes your ego can get in the way of allowing things to organically unfold. Maybe Oprah would have focused on the rest of the guests later in the show. Perhaps she needed to gush over the ABC stars first so she could turn her focus and attention to all of us. I have no way of knowing for sure. I don't regret walking off the set that day, but I have since learned not to let my ego drive my judgment. As the old saying goes, "You catch more flies with honey than you do with vinegar!"

I'm just sayin'!

CHAPTER THIRTEEN

Success Is the Best Revenge

When I first attended the Daytime Emmys back in 1983, the ceremony took place in the afternoon, which made sense, seeing as it was all about daytime shows. The event was usually held in the ballroom of one of New York's biggest hotels, like the Waldorf Astoria or the Sheraton. Everyone typically sat at round tables with people from their show, and the awards were presented as we ate a lovely meal and drank fine wine and champagne. Since there was very little room left to sell tickets to the fans, there were typically only a select few in attendance; it was really just the daytime community in attendance, celebrating that year's excellence.

Those afternoons were so much fun because there was no time limit on the winners' speeches. It was always an added special treat when people went up to accept their awards later in the show, after they had been enjoying wine all afternoon. Those who had had one too many rambled on and on for what seemed like forever, but their speeches were always the most enjoyable.

The way the daytime nominees were selected is kind of interesting. First each soap opera conducted an in-house ballot in which we were asked as a cast to pick two or three nominees in each category. The top two vote getters in each category would be submitted to the academy and put on the official ballot. Then the whole daytime community voted (actors for actors, directors for directors, etc.), and the top five vote getters became the official nominees. The nominees then had to submit a reel of their best work from the year, to be judged by a volunteer panel of actors, directors, producers, and others who were members of the National Academy of Television Arts & Sciences. In those days, an actor could submit three episodes, but the rub was that you had to submit complete episodes. Every scene you were in had to be included, whether you had ninety lines or one. Nothing could be edited out of your scenes, although you were allowed to delete scenes you weren't in.

Luckily, when I received my first nomination in 1985, I had a fantastic year of material to choose from. I thought it was important to show that Reva was both funny and emotional. She could make her audience laugh and cry—in the same scene! It wasn't because I was a brilliant actress. Nope. It was all about the stellar writing on the show and how well my character was developed—even before I breathed life into her on-screen.

I actually had a hard time putting together a reel of my work, because there were so many good episodes to choose from. This was the year of my infamous "fountain scene," where I stripped down to my undies and baptized myself the "Slut of Springfield" in front of Josh. But guess what—that wasn't on my reel! The fountain scene happened at the very end of the episode, which mainly consisted of one big party scene with the entire cast. I may have had a funny line here and a snippy line there, but there was no real "meat" until that last scene. Admittedly, it was a doozy, but I was afraid voters would get bored watching the party scenes and wouldn't get to the final fountain scene before casting a "no" vote.

I can't remember exactly what *was* on my reel that year, but I know it had a lot to do with the fabulous Lewis men! My husband helped me a lot when it came time to choose the episodes for my Emmy reel. I cut the choices down to about ten episodes, and I'd handcuff him to the sofa and make him watch each one until we made our final choices. I was sometimes too close to the material to be unbiased, but A.C. always had an amazing eye for what would grab a vote in my favor. When I was nominated in 1998, the Year of the Clone, I used the episode where Dolly has overdosed on the "rapid aging serum" and Dolly and Reva talk about life as Dolly ages and dies in Reva's arms! Sounds like a *Saturday Night Live* skit, but it was actually very moving and emotional. I had asked A.C. and our son Max to watch the episode to see if I should submit it to the Emmy nominating committee. Well, when I walked back in the room, they were both in tears! It was so sweet watching two grown men trying to hide the fact that they were crying because Dolly was dead! That convinced me that I should use it! (Susan Lucci won that year. . . . Oh, well.) But that first year, I used a very emotional episode first, then picked something outrageously funny second (thank you, Pam and Jeff), and then went for heavy-duty drama for the third. You know, that good old-fashioned chest-beating, tear-flowing *Guiding Light* episode!

I was up against the heavy hitters from other daytime shows, including Susan Lucci, Deidre Hall, Robin Strasser, who was on *One Life to Live* when I was there, and Gillian Spencer. I knew all of their work and was a fan of each one. I was definitely the dark horse in the race that year, as I had been on *Guiding Light* for less than two seasons. I know it sounds clichéd to say, but it was simply an honor to be nominated. It was also extremely special because Larry Gates, who played H. B. Lewis, was nominated in the Best Supporting Actor category that same year. At the time, Reva was married to H.B., so it was a total joy for me to share this experience with Larry.

I wasn't expected to win. After all, given my competition and the fact that nobody really knew who I was, really, who would have guessed? I was the newbie on the scene. Although the press had dubbed me "the dark horse who was going to win," I didn't give it a shot in hell. Still, I was giddy with excitement and wanted to drink the entire first-time experience in—especially because I had no way of knowing how long Reva would last. This could have been my one trip to the ball! I brought my entire family to New York City for my big day. My husband, my sister, and her husband and my parents were all there to cheer me on. I was so happy to have everyone there to share in the experience. We decided to make the event a real party. We took a black stretch limousine from our home in New Jersey to the show, which was at the famed Waldorf Astoria hotel that year. I usually rode the bus to work, so hiring a limo was a real splurge, and I will readily admit it was a complete luxury.

I dressed in a funky getup that was typical 1980s chic: an oversequined, low-cut, big-shouldered white top with pink sequined flowers and a short white leather skirt. That top was so ugly, but at the time, I loved it! I wore six-inch white patent-leather stilettos and "put-ons," which are clip-on hair extensions clipped into my actual hair. They came in all different colors and were really fun to wear. I had done a magazine shoot for the company who made the extensions, and when I received my nomination, they immediately offered to do my hair. I was thrilled because I pictured myself as the white Patti LaBelle. I said yes, thinking that at the very least I would garner some press for my hair, since I was certain I wasn't going to win.

On the big day, I had a giant fan of hair extensions sticking straight up from my head. I thought I looked amazing. They were beautiful, but let's just say not terribly functional. When my name was unexpectedly announced as the winner, I could hardly believe what I had heard. And then one overwhelming thought raced through my mind: *Oh, my God! What have I done to my hair?*

I kissed my husband and anyone else sitting near me as I burst into tears of joy. I ran toward the stage, leaving a trail of hair extensions behind me. They were falling out with every step I took. And, as if that wasn't bad enough, one of my shoes flipped off my foot, so I took the other one off too and threw them into the air in celebration. As I began to speak, I realized I hadn't prepared anything to say. So I did what any seasoned actress would do—I ad-libbed! To be completely honest, I was one of those long ramblers the first year I won.

Being recognized by my peers amid that level of talent in other soaps was an amazing, unforgettable thrill—winning was simply the icing on the big, chocolaty cake! And let's not forget that I won that first Emmy a year and a half after being fired from *One Life to Live*. After the awards show, the vice president of daytime for ABC actually threw her arm around my shoulders and told me how happy she was that ABC had "discovered" me.

Hello?

I had already been on *The Doctors* for *four* years!

"Sure, you discovered me and then you fired me," I said. "I went to another show and won an Emmy!" I guess I could have added, *Put that in your pipe and smoke it*, but decided not to.

Who, me?

Burn bridges?

Naw!

As the old saying goes, "Success is the best revenge."

On my first day back on the set after I won, we were shooting yet another party scene. Reva, who was from the "wrong side of the tracks," was now married to H. B. Lewis, and she wanted to fit in with all of the hot power women of Springfield. The scene we were shooting opened with all of the hoity-toity women sitting around a table in the country club, including the wonderful Beverlee McKinsey, Maeve Kincaid, and Mary Kay Adams. Reva always knew how to make an entrance, and this charity event was no exception. She blew through the door and plopped herself down at their table like she was one of them. All I was supposed to say was something like "You all have to accept me now because I am Reva Shayne and I am married to H. B. Lewis. I belong at this table!"

The problem was that I was so excited by my Emmy win that I couldn't get a single line right. I knew what I was supposed to say but I bobbled my dialogue for eight straight takes. After my eighth flub, Beverlee looked right at me and, as cool as can be in her oozing Southern accent, said, "You give the girl an Emmy and she can't remember a fucking line!"

My second Emmy win came in 1987. I had just given birth to my son Max and wasn't feeling quite ready to be in something slinky. I decided on a sleeveless sequined blue dress that gave me a little breathing room. At this point my hair was cut really short, so there wasn't much I could do to mess it up this time! Compared to my first Emmy win, I looked downright conservative and yet a bit trashy all at the same time; I had no bra on and was still nursing Max, so my breasts were racktacular!

When you are nominated in the category of Outstanding Leading Actress in a Daytime Series, you can count on one thing: You will always be up against the very best in the business. But this time, I actually thought I had a real shot at winning, because the material I picked that year was outstanding. If the voters did what they were supposed to do by voting strictly on the material submitted and not on a character's or actor's popularity, I knew I was going to be hard to beat. That year, Reva appeared as a character in a book that one of the other characters on the show was writing. She was portrayed as a chanteuse in a 1920s cabaret. The scene was shot in black-and-white, which gave it a vintage feel. I was allowed to sing and shimmy along to "How Come You Do Me Like You Do." (Kudos to anyone reading this book who remembers that song!) When they showed this clip during the Emmys, out of context, I thought maybe it looked a bit silly. Nominees don't know what clips the Emmy producers will choose to use during the show, so it is always a surprise—even for us. When I saw the clip that night, I was a little embarrassed, yet still really happy knowing how good my work was that season. I realize some actors cannot look at their work—I am not one of those people. I was an avid watcher of the show, whether my scenes were a part of that particular episode or not.

I was nominated with Elizabeth Hubbard, Susan Lucci, Frances Reid, and Marcy Walker. When the wonderfully talented David Canary called out my name, I was far more composed than I had been for my first win. Still, I cried and got emotional; I don't know how anyone can help it! I also forgot to thank my husband, so, A.C., please know that I thank you for all of your love and support—then, now, and always!

My third Emmy win came in 1990—the year I was leaving *Guiding Light*. Other nominees that year included Susan Lucci, Elizabeth Hubbard, Finola Hughes, and Jeanne Cooper. It was a bittersweet victory, because I didn't know whether I'd ever have another opportunity to work in daytime, let alone stand in front of a room of my peers being honored for my work. In my acceptance speech that night, I thanked the academy for giving me three awards, one for each of my children.

I also mentioned I was leaving the show. The next day, there was a memorable headline in the soap opera press that read, "Never say never. Zimmer will be back!" I guess you could say they knew something I didn't, because when I announced that I was leaving *Guiding Light*, I truly had no intention of ever going back to the show.

But, of course, I did come back. And in 2006, after eleven nominations throughout my career, I won my fourth Emmy. This was the most special to me, as this was the one I would keep for myself, as I always envisioned my first three Emmys someday going to my children. Now that I had a fourth, I could be buried with it if I wanted to!

And I had never expected to win. Each one of my Emmy awards represents a portion of Reva's life that I am extremely proud to have been a part of. 2006 was mostly devoted to Reva's menopause story, which I didn't feel was our best. It went no-where. When I look back on this win, I can honestly say that I did not win the Emmy; we, as a show, did!

Having four Emmy awards is a great honor. And to some, it is also a tempting curiosity—especially when it came to my chil-dren and their friends. I keep my Emmys on display on top of a wardrobe in our living room, visible to anyone who walks by. When Rachel turned sixteen, she decided to have a party. She invited only a handful of kids, but once the word spread that there was a party, those kids invited other kids and we ended up with a lot more people than we were expecting, including a bunch of kids we didn't recognize.

Fortunately, A.C. and I were home, so things couldn't get too out of hand. We did our best not to be the "buttinskis" and *mostly* stayed upstairs and out of sight so our daughter and her friends could have a good time. But every now and then one of us would make our way downstairs for one reason or another so we could check things out without being too obvious. On one of those trips, I noticed that one of my Emmys was missing.

I dashed upstairs to tell A.C.

"I don't want to cause an alarm, but one of my Emmys is missing," I said.

"What are you talking about?" He was incensed that some-one would come into our home and swipe, of all things, my Emmy! Like we wouldn't notice that the golden statue was miss-ing?

We wanted to make sure that someone hadn't just picked it up to admire it and misplaced it somewhere else, so we searched the house high and low. It was definitely gone. Before I could blink, A.C. had gone out to our garage and gotten a broken spade that now looked like a giant walking stick. He walked around the party like Sheriff Buford Pusser from *Walking Tall*, and started interrogating the kids. "We've had something stolen from the house. Nobody is leaving until someone tells me if they know anything."

A.C. was so mad. None of the kids wanted to be on the receiving end of that awful can of whoop-ass he was about crack open. One by one, he brought suspicious-looking kids into our living room.

"Who are you? . . . What school do you go to? . . . What are your parents' names and numbers? . . . Did you take or do you know anything about my wife's missing Emmy?"

Most of the kids had no idea what an Emmy is or looks like. It was pretty clear they didn't have a clue. A.C.'s questioning went on for an hour, until he made each of the kids call their parents to come pick them up. The ones we didn't know had already fled on foot!

I began sobbing, which started a landslide of tears as Rachel began to cry too. She was so embarrassed and appalled at the same time. She didn't know most of the kids who were there, so it wasn't like one of her friends had done this. She felt that someone she didn't know had ruined her sixteenth-birthday party. I felt awful for her.

We ended up calling the police so we could fill out a robbery report. They dusted for fingerprints, but the effort was futile, given the number of people who had come and gone that night. I was certain I would never see that award again.

The next day, I received a phone call from a befuddled guy who had gone outside to fetch his morning paper and found my Emmy award on his front porch. He recognized my name on the brass plaque at the bottom and figured I must be missing it. Apparently, his daughter's boyfriend had taken it from our house and left it at their doorstep for the girl, who was an aspiring actress, as an inspiration to pursue her dreams. He left a note that read, *You are the best actress I know. Here's an Emmy.*

In my melodramatic mind, I thought his gesture was actually sweet and romantic. In the end, we decided not to press charges against the young man, hoping he learned his lesson. I had my Emmy back, and to me, that was the happiest ending I could have hoped for.

With four Emmy wins over the years, after ten nominations, there were also six Emmy losses. People always wonder how it feels to lose. Is it devastating? Do you go home and cry or rant at the unfairness? Honestly, I felt a sense of relief wash over me whenever my name wasn't called, because it meant I didn't have to make some charming, funny, or poignant acceptance speech. It also meant that I wouldn't have to face the reporters in the back room who never really wanted to know how I felt about winning so much as how it felt to beat Susan Lucci . . . again! I didn't think it was gracious for the press to focus on Susan's loss while interviewing me about my win. Still, I was the one holding the statue that night, and you know what? That felt really great.

After Susan had been nominated a dozen or so times without winning, the awards show and all the publicity became centered on whether or not her losing streak would be broken. She actually got more mileage out of losing the Emmy than she ever did from winning it! In 1998, the year she finally won, I decided to splurge on several six-hundred-dollar tickets to the show so my children could attend with A.C. and me. A lot of people were saying that it was my year to win it because of the clone story that everyone supposedly hated so much!

Rachel was fifteen, Max was eleven, and Jake was eight years old. I thought it would be fun for them to experience the excitement of an awards show. We settled into our seats at the Theatre inside Madison Square Garden for the broadcast. Wayne Gretzky and his beautiful wife, Janet, were sitting right in front of us. The boys were so excited to see the "Great One."

As awards shows often do, the evening wore on and the children started to get antsy. My category of Lead Actress was always announced near the end of the evening. When Shemar Moore announced that the winner was Susan Lucci, my boys jumped out of their seats and at the tops of their lungs started yelling, "You've got to be kidding! My mom was robbed!" Although I appreciated their enthusiasm, thank God the ovation for Susan was deafening and no one but Wayne and Janet could hear what my sons were screaming! They turned around and said politely, "We think so too!" I'm sure they didn't mean it and were just being nice to my kids. I'm sure they, like everyone there, were thrilled for Susan. And to be totally honest, I was happy for her too. Every time I've had the pleasure of being in Susan's company, she has always been gracious, kind, and lovely. Her husband, Helmut, is a doll too.

The year I won my fourth Emmy, my son Max was watching the ceremony at a sports bar with some teammates from his college football team. Here were these big, burly guys who had probably never even watched my show, cheering me on like I was their second mom. Max told me that when they announced my name as the winner, they all started jumping around like a bunch of cheerleaders. Winning that Emmy was especially delicious because three of my costars, Tom Pelphrey, Gina Tognoni, and Jordan Clarke, also took home trophies that night!

CHAPTER FOURTEEN

Don't Call Me Diva!

have always had a reputation for being blatantly honest with my fans in interviews and with my coworkers on the set. If I didn't like something, I said how I felt. There were people who believed my irreverence was an asset, and those who, well, didn't. There were many times throughout my career when I'd be giving an interview and the publicist for the show would step in and say, "Are you sure you want to say it like *that*?" Publicists always had to remain on their toes with me, because they were never sure what was going to come out of my mouth next.

What I've learned over the years is that you're damned if you do and damned if you don't, so I figure I might as well speak the truth—if only my truth. Holding my feelings inside gave the fans the opportunity to call me out, especially if they didn't agree with either a decision I personally made or a decision about the direction of my character, which was mostly out of my hands. My fans had become accustomed to me speaking out, so when something happened that they didn't like, they expected me to say something. Sometimes, though, I didn't. If bitching about it didn't benefit me or the direction the character was going in, if it was too late to stop the building from burning anyway, if the damage had already been done—speaking out wouldn't have made a difference.

Fans like to be told the truth, because life isn't all roses and champagne.

Nope.

Sometimes you've got to have a little Jack Daniel's mixed in there for good measure. Sometimes you can take the high road and suck it up, and other times, you've got to take a shot of whiskey and do what you have to do.

I love honesty.

That's who I am to my core.

I'm just sayin'!

So, here goes. What I am about to tell you is my version of what happened behind the scenes that ultimately killed *Guiding Light*. For better or for worse, this is the way I saw things.

I loved my job.

I worked really hard at it to make my career everything it could possibly be and so I could get the most joy and pleasure out of every blessed moment. Being an actress came easily to me, and for years, I never had a worry about my future or career. During the last five years of *Guiding Light*, everything changed.

It's my opinion that 2004 was the beginning of the end. With our ratings down (like those of most soap operas), the executives at Procter & Gamble responded in two ways: by changing our leadership and by cutting our budget. They wanted new producers and writers and they wanted to save money, to do things as cheaply as possible. Our production budget plummeted.

Our new executive producer was Ellen Wheeler. I had heard only great things about Ellen from others who knew her. Before making her shift to behind the camera, first as a director and then as a line producer, she had been an actress; in fact, she had won two Emmy awards as an actress for her work on *All My Children* and then on *Another World*. Her background reminded me of that of my husband, who also got bored with acting and wanted to branch out and do other things. It was my hope that she would bring a fresh new perspective to the look of the show because it was in dire need of some new energy, and she had it. I knew she was a well-liked director because she was able to get things done at a quick pace, a real asset in the world of daytime television. Actors love directors who can get the job done, and with her experience as a daytime actor, I thought she'd be able to offer up some good advice.

One funny thing was that when Ellen came on board, it was the first time I had a boss who was actually younger than me. It was weird—like going to a new doctor who is younger than you. Something about that just doesn't feel right. Here I had just turned fifty and the suits at Procter & Gamble brought in a young whippersnapper to be my new boss. It was just another painful reminder that everyone can be replaced with someone younger and cheaper.

Another difference was that all of my former executive producers were men who in many ways had been like father figures to me. I hadn't had a female executive producer since the early days of my career, when I was a perfect size six, hadn't had any babies yet, and still had my rapid metabolism. I always thought of myself as an actress who didn't need to be a perfect size six, but the truth is that for years, I didn't actually have to watch my weight. Sure, there were a few executive producers throughout my career who let me know they thought I was getting a little chubby or I was getting jowls and should think about getting a face-lift. My bigger problem was that as my waistline expanded, our wardrobe designer had a hell of a time trying to dress me!

He knew how to dress sizes two, four, six, and eight, but not the twelves and fourteens. And he wouldn't be caught dead in the chubby-girl stores! A lot of the girls on the show used to swear that our wardrobe department purposely shrank our clothes so we'd get extremely paranoid and feel like we had to lose weight. I wasn't sure what Ellen would think of me when she came on board, but I was initially excited to have her there. I figured that as a woman, she would be more forgiving of my weight gain. At least, I was hoping so.

I got along with Ellen in the beginning, but deep down, I think I was a little bit jealous of her. I never had any desire to do anything other than act, but people often told me they thought I'd make a great producer. An executive producer's job is to oversee the production—budgets, schedules, hiring, and all other aspects of a show, including the general direction of the story. Good executive producers guide the show with their vision of what they want the show to be, while letting their writers write, their directors direct, and their actors act.

Well, I think it is fair to say that Ellen didn't understand the show or my character Reva like I did, having spent close to twenty years there before she took over. When she came on board, numerous changes were made to the sets, the stories, and the cast. That was when I felt everything began to really fall apart. I was miserable because they were tinkering with my character, and it was even worse because my entire life had gone through a shift. My children were all grown and living their own lives away from home. Work was the focus and center of my life, so anything that threatened this existence didn't go over well with me.

After Ellen took over the reins, several veteran actors were dropped from the show because of budget cuts. Without contracts, their salaries were no longer guaranteed. They became day players or heavy recurring characters. Still, without their contracts in place, several chose to leave the show to find steadier work. Maureen Garrett, who played Holly, Jerry verDorn, who played Ross Marler, and Marj Dusay, who played Alexandra Spaulding, were just a few of the actors who left the show after Ellen chose to take them off contract, meaning they were no longer guaranteed a weekly salary. With these actors gone, there was a lack of veteran influence, allowing Ellen to refocus the show on the youth of Springfield. I believe she was well-intentioned. She wanted to be the white knight who saved *Guiding Light*, but why reinvent the wheel, trying to turn the show into something it was never meant to be? In my opinion, it was a losing proposition to buck the formula that had been successful for, at that point, sixty-eight very solid years.

Ellen was so set on reinventing the show that she lost the connection we all once felt. She wanted to make it hip, edgy, and cool so it would appeal to a younger demographic. The problem with that concept was that those traits didn't play with our fans who had been watching for thirty, forty, or fifty years! I'm just sayin'! They liked the show as it was—comfortable and familiar.

While Ellen was busy blazing her new trail, she didn't stand a chance against my growing anger and disappointment with the changes that were happening to the show. Although I would have been angry regardless, I honestly believe a male executive producer would have been able to keep me in line a little better than Ellen did during those years.

In my mind, Ellen's hiring was Procter & Gamble's way of making it clear they wanted out of *Guiding Light*, and they figured there was only one way to do it: drive the show's remaining fans away forever. To do that, to pull off this disaster, Procter & Gamble needed complicit employees. They had that in Ellen. It seemed to me as if they were intent on producing their version of *Springtime for Hitler* and hoping for a failure.

Ellen was terrific at bringing the whole cast and crew together for meetings that gave the impression that we were all a team. I liked that idea, because I have always been a real team player. But even though I couldn't put my finger on it at first, there was always something a little bit off about those meetings. It didn't take long to see that Ellen was an ambitious woman who wasn't happy just being the executive producer; she needed to put her stamp *all over* the show. When the writer's strike hit Hollywood, she not only produced and directed—she got to write *Guiding Light* too. Even though the executives had stocked up on scripts by asking the writers to double and triple up on their work, Ellen found herself in the position of writing a show she otherwise wouldn't have been allowed to write for (because she wasn't in the Writers Guild). I always knew which scripts were our writers' and which were Ellen's. You see, all executive producers have their favorite characters, and it appeared that Ellen was no exception. What hurt me was that I felt Reva was not one of them. In fact, Reva was actually placed on the back burner. Fans noticed the shift and wrote in to say they wanted more Reva. That was hard for me, because I wasn't used to letting the fans down.

I am the first to admit that a daytime drama is not an island.

It is a collection of talent. No single person can be expected to carry the entire show—on-screen or behind the scenes. Going back to the early days of the show, *Guiding Light* always had the best cast and crew in television. But now there were several cast members who became frustrated by the changes of our new regime. Many of us didn't think that Ellen listened to the problems we had with the direction a character was going, the way a story was developing, or the entire tone of the show. She and her team seemed to enjoy breaking up well-established "supercouples," belittling relationships that the audience had invested in for years. I'm talking about Harley and Gus—and most especially the debacle of Josh and Cassie!

I understand that Ellen had a job to do, that her marching orders were to save money and produce the show as cheaply as possible. She was the paid hatchet who came in to chop whatever fat from the bottom line she could. And she succeeded.

In an odd way, I admired her tenacity and willingness to put herself on the line the way she did. I wouldn't say the demise of the show was her fault or a result of the decisions she made so much as I think it was about changing times and the ratings decline that all of daytime was experiencing. Many factors contributed to the suits' final decision to take us off the air. Who knows? Maybe in another situation at another time, I would have adored working for Ellen. But because I realized that all of these changes were leading to the end of *Guiding Light*, working on the show while Ellen was in charge was, by far, the hardest experience of my professional career.

I always hated the word *diva* because in my mind it meant someone who was selfish or unreasonable. But in the daytime world, *diva* really just means you've achieved a certain level of success—if not respect. Although I played one on television, I am not totally convinced I was an actual daytime diva. I wasn't hard to work with; at least, I don't think I was—and I don't think the suits would have described me as hard to work with either; but they might tell you I could be impatient, tough, and a real ball breaker. And you know what? They'd be right.

Ellen and I had some pretty good blowouts over the years. When people saw me headed for the fifth floor of the studio to have a meeting with her, everyone in the vicinity usually disappeared. One of the writer's assistants on the show once told me that whenever Ellen got a phone message that Zimmer wanted to talk, she said, "Oh, boy. This must be serious." I believe that writers were paid to do a certain job, and my role as an actress was to let them do it without lots of input from me. I didn't want the blame if something didn't work on the page, same as they didn't want to take the blame if I botched a scene on-screen. Those poor writers took shit about stories and characters all the time. They had enough on their plate without one of us actors butting in with our two cents all the time.

So I didn't bitch lightly, and everything I bitched about was in the best interest of the show. There were plenty of times I walked out of Ellen's office when I am sure she was left asking herself, *Who does she think she is, coming in here and talking to me like that?* And no question, there were lots of times my complaining was rooted in my ego. I didn't like being put on the back burner. If I wasn't in an episode for a few days, I'd march right up to the fifth floor and demand an explanation. I always gave Ellen the opportunity to justify her decisions, but I rarely changed my mind about how they made me feel. I'd sit and listen, while she usually cried. The more she cried, the more I wanted to lay into her. She was the executive producer of a show that was struggling to stay afloat, and all she could do was cry? C'mon! There's no crying in daytime.

Well, okay. You got me. There's *lots* of crying in daytime, but on-screen, not behind the scenes! And that was the problem in a nutshell. When the curtain came down at the end of the day, too many of us were crying.

CHAPTER FIFTEEN

Seventy Years Strong and We Were Dying

pick up the

uiding Light celebrated its seventieth anniversary in 2007. Ellen had all sorts of interesting ideas to commemorate this tremendous milestone, and she brought many of the actors into her office to get their suggestions too. One of the concepts she had was to interview each of us on where or how we found our "light" in life and tack our short vignettes onto the end of each episode. I actually loved this concept! It was a nice addition to hear the actors talk about special moments in their real lives.

With the growing popularity of reality television, Ellen also came up with an idea to do episodes that focused on specific characters so the viewers could spend "a day in the life of . . ." their favorites from the show. We loved doing those episodes because they allowed the viewer to get an intimate peek into the lives of our characters, the little idiosyncrasies of their day-to-day life. They got to watch Reva brush her teeth, pick up the morning paper from the driveway, and all of the other little things we all do without a thought.

Of course, the actors also loved these episodes because we got to star in our own one-hour show. For that day, it was all about us. Even though these episodes took the viewer out of the forward motion of the plot, they were interesting and entertaining and, I will admit, innovative and creative.

Reva's day-in-the-life took place on the day that Josh and Reva were going to finalize their divorce. The show opened with Reva waking up and making herself coffee, getting her morning paper, showering, and then looking down at her hands and her wedding band, which she was still wearing. The audience knew she was going to take it off at some point during the day, because this was the day she would be divorced from her soul mate.

This particular episode also showed Robert Newman's character, Josh, as he went through his own morning routine. We followed Josh and Reva leading up to the moment they were supposed to sign their divorce papers, and the episode ended with them running off together to the Springfield lighthouse, where they decided not to get divorced after all. They tore up the documents so there would be no chance of going through with it. I thought the show was extremely powerful. Even though it focused on these two characters, the writers were able to move the story along—something that is critical in daytime dramas.

As another way to celebrate the seventieth anniversary, Ellen created a *Guiding Light* Gives Back campaign, where the show could show its appreciation for its fans. One of her ideas was to take the entire cast to Biloxi, Mississippi, in the aftermath of Hurricane Katrina to tape a special episode in which we helped to rebuild homes with a group called the HandsOn Network. Ellen thought it would be interesting to see the actors, as themselves, doing the work, as opposed to our characters. She wanted to air the show in place of a regular episode of *Guiding Light*. Even though I loved the idea of helping the people in Biloxi, this episode would be breaking what is often referred to as the "fourth wall."

Breaking the fourth wall is when a character speaks directly to the audience through the camera in a film or television program. People tune in to see their favorite characters—not the actors playing those characters. I firmly believed that the line between fantasy and reality would be crossed if we did this show.

I didn't want to appear as someone who didn't care about the people who were affected by the devastation of Hurricane Katrina, but I felt so strongly about not breaking character that I initially refused to go on the trip. I was in the minority; most of the cast were eager to go to Mississippi to help in any way they could.

When Ellen called me into her office to ask why I didn't want to take the trip with the rest of the cast, I was honest. "If the episode airs in the *Guiding Light* time slot, I am no longer Reva Shayne—I'm Kim Zimmer." I thought I had a good point. I had been playing Reva a lot longer than Ellen had been around. I didn't think it was a smart decision for the show or my character.

Lots of meetings took place before it was decided that the episode would be shot but would air only as a Web series on a *Guiding Light*–inspired Web site, findyourlight.net. By the time that decision was made, I had researched HandsOn Network and realized this could be a wonderful project, so I agreed to go along. To me, the shift to the webcast gave the project more meaning and allowed us the freedom to be ourselves. When I went back to tell Ellen I had changed my mind and would like to be a part of the Biloxi project, she was so happy that she actually broke down in tears. Truth be told, Ellen Wheeler cried more often than Reva Shayne. Still, it meant a lot to me that she was so moved by my change of heart.

When we arrived, we were split into teams to work on four different houses. The homes had already undergone mold remediation by the folks from HandsOn, which I can only imagine was not a pleasant job. Once the houses had been prepared, it was our turn to team up with experienced people from HandsOn to prep the houses for Sheetrock and drywall!

Biloxi turned out to be the most incredible experience for all of us. Since we were a bunch of actors, not construction workers, they offered us a tutorial before we actually got started. We had to sign a release saying we were allowed to operate tools and machinery. When I showed the document to my husband before I signed it, he said, "Where do I write that under any and all circumstances, you are not allowed to use power tools!"

A lot of guys on our show had worked construction as a way to supplement their income. And Beth Chamberlin, the beautiful actress who played Beth Raines Spaulding, had renovated her home and knew how to use every power tool they had in the box—and then some! I could swing a hammer and hit the head of a nail with pretty good precision, and knew how to use a nail gun without hurting anyone else, so my role was pretty well-defined. By the end of the week, however, I also knew how to use a circular saw and put up drywall!

It was moving and refreshing to be a part of this important community service. We got to know the neighborhood and the people who lived in it. One memorable woman shared with me her story of survival after the hurricane hit. She explained that her refrigerator saved her life; it tipped over as her kitchen was filling up with water, so she was able to climb on top, punch a hole in her ceiling, and climb out onto the roof, where she could be rescued. Another woman told me how she was able to climb up a tree as her wheelchair got washed away. By the grace of God, another wheelchair came floating by. She was able to grab on to it and hold it until she too could be rescued. Their stories of survival were nothing short of miraculous and inspiring. All the people we met along the way were completely unforgettable.

We ended up building four homes in Biloxi during our stay. I witnessed uninhabitable, mold-infested houses become brand-new cozy homes. Procter & Gamble paid to furnish the homes, and the many sponsors of the event jumped on board to pitch in too. It was a really great bonding experience for all of us. We became a crew of people working together toward one common goal.

Interestingly, that week turned out to be the closest I ever felt to Ellen. We had some of the warmest, most sincere and honest conversations we'd ever had. Ellen was always guarded when we interacted back in New York, but I found her to be open and available in Biloxi. That week made me question everything I had felt about her prior to our trip. When all was said and done, she worked her ass off down there. She made the whole thing happen. And I felt guilty about trash-talking her or ever thinking I shouldn't go or that airing the show on *Guiding Light* was a bad idea. I still believe that my initial judgment was correct, but no question: The end result was brilliant. In addition, the fan reaction was amazing, so it turned out to be a very positive experience for all involved.

It had been three years since Ellen came on board as the executive producer. Despite our continued low ratings, *Guiding Light* won the Emmy award for Best Writing and Best Show in 2007. We actually tied with *The Young and the Restless* for Best Show, but hey, a win is a win, right? Truthfully, though, I didn't really understand the kudos for the show; I felt it was dying a slow and painful death, just like many an ill-fated character in the ever-changing but always dramatic world of daytime television.

Anyway, I heard that Ellen decided it would be a swell idea to kick off 2008 with a new look for the show. In our seventy-first season of broadcasting, she replaced the anniversary opening with a new show opening and the rumor was that she wanted to launch this campaign by calling the show *The New Guiding Light*. The first show of the new year would be "episode one"—were we supposed to just erase the more than fifteen thousand episodes that came before? I don't think so!

To me, *Guiding Light* was an heirloom and a treasure. I was proud of the legacy that had been created by all of the actors who came before me, and the contributions I had made to the show over the years.

I knew very well how much the suits hated it when people talked about how old *Guiding Light* was. I recall one of them protesting that it was like calling a woman an old broad past her. But recognizing our history wasn't calling the show old! *Guiding Light* wasn't an old broad; it was a legend, like Elizabeth Taylor or Sophia Loren. And now the powers that be wanted to throw that legacy out and start all over with "episode one"?

Except for some of the brand-new actors on the show, everyone on the set was in shock at the notion of wiping out the history of our show. The new actors didn't care; they had a job that was paying them more money than they had ever made in their lives. They were living the good life in their nice apartments in Manhattan and knew nothing of the long history of our show. It was just a job for them. As much as I would have loved to be that naive and able to let it go, I couldn't.

Thank God Procter & Gamble took a stand and said, "Absolutely not!"

While the rest of us were relieved, Ellen did succeed in keeping the new opening for the show, however: a bunch of hairy-ass arms reaching and grabbing at other hairy-ass arms! With a series of voice-overs uttering the famous line, "There is a destiny. . . ." You know the one!

This happened right around the same time that the executives decided to change the entire look of our show. They said they wanted to create a more "realistic" experience for the viewer. So *Guiding Light* became the first American daytime soap to be shot entirely on handheld digital cameras. These were portable and less cumbersome than the traditional pedestal-style studio cameras used for decades. The handheld cameras allowed producers to choose many different locations and gave them the flexibility to shoot as they wished without a lot of time-consuming setup.

The suits also decided to spend a small fortune that I didn't think they had to, to replace all the sets on the show with permanent four-sided sets with ceilings to make it look more realistic! This way, they no longer had to worry about shooting on location or catching lights in the grid overhead because there were no ceilings. The permanent sets had ceilings and were self-contained, separate rooms that stayed dressed all of the time. Our former sets had moving walls and interchangeable elements, which meant they had to be taken down every night and set back up each morning, depending on which sets were being used for the episode that day. This meant two crews working around the clock—a day crew and a night crew. That was a major expense that was eliminated with the new permanent sets.

Though it was a real coup for our set designer (I have to say that he did a brilliant job of design), the four-sided sets were way too small, and hotter than blue blazes because of the lack of ventilation. Say your scene took place in the set for Vanessa's hotel suite; you had to share that tiny space with three camera-men, two people holding light poles, and one or two sound guys holding boom mics to record the dialogue. And this small army didn't include anyone else who was in the scene with you. A simple direction to walk across the room meant negotiating your way around all these people on the set, and making it look like they weren't there. That was when we all really got to know our colleagues well, including what everyone had had for lunch or dinner the night before, if you catch my literal drift!

As part of the new look of our show, Ellen introduced the "shaky cam," a style of shooting that is often used in films and associated with extreme close-ups. This style of camera work proved to be disorienting for viewers, who were used to the more traditional look of soap operas.

The straw that broke the camel's back came in February 2008, when they decided that in addition to our New York studio, they could save even more money, and gain lots of options for locations and scenery, by shooting outside of Manhattan, in Peapack, New Jersey. The show house contained permanent sets, while *Guiding Light*'s production offices were dressed and re-dressed as motel rooms, nail salons, a Quik Mart, or anything the show called for that day. For example, Ellen's office doubled as a chapel, complete with an altar and pews. If you had a meeting with Ellen, you had to sit in the pews. She either sat in the pews with you or at her desk, which was out of sight behind the altar. God bless us, everyone!

One of the other offices housed the Cedars Hospital's gynecology office. "Excuse us, but could you take your work to another desk for the next hour? We need to shoot Reva's prenatal examination in here!" I'm not kidding! It was odd and uncomfortable for all of us.

Not to mention that half the time, we were shuttling around New Jersey to shoot in various locations. The idea of shooting outside was exciting when it was first presented to us. We were told that they wanted to make the show "edgier, more MTV, more *Friday Night Lights*." Unfortunately, the resulting lighting and sound from that point forward were awful. If you were one of the few people still watching our show at that time, you probably noticed the lack in production value. Instead of looking cool and fresh, we ended up looking like cable access! I had seen better amateur videos posted on YouTube! Costumes, hair, and makeup were all impacted too, because not only were the budgets for those departments cut, but there was now a lack of time to make hair and makeup changes, because we started shooting so much material for several episodes at a time in a single day at a single location. It was cruel and unusual punishment for a fifty-three-year-old woman to be shot that real and raw. I had no idea I could ever look so bad!

Okay. Just so you hear what I'm sayin'. . . Procter & Gamble, one of the most successful corporations in the world, claimed it was too expensive to maintain a studio in New York. And their solution was to force the actors out into the cold to a house in Peapack, and then turn everything into a location shoot. This was patently wrong and made as little sense as one of our far-fetched soap stories.

I became obsessed with the quickly declining quality of our show. I'd campaign to anyone who would listen, trying to get them to see my perspective. I watched the show every single day. If I didn't watch it live, I recorded it. And if that wasn't enough to fill my already overflowing plate, I made it a point to watch other soaps too so I could see how they were being shot.

"Did you see today's show? It was the biggest piece of shit. It was dreck from beginning to end!"

Most of the actors told me they had stopped watching two or more years ago. "You'd be wise to stop watching it too. Why do you do that to yourself?" they'd ask.

I didn't have a good answer, except that I was so emotionally attached that it was hard for me to let it go. I wasn't just an actress on *Guiding Light*—I was also a fan. I admired everybody's work. We had such a talented group of people working on our show. I deeply cared about the show—maybe to a fault.

The focus had shifted from producing great television to getting it done as fast as we could. The emphasis was no longer on the stories being told but how fast we could get those stories "in the can."

I remember the day we were shooting the *Josh and Reva: A Love Story* film within the show. We were shooting outside under big trees when a huge thunderstorm started to blow through.

I for one knew that where there was thunder, there was lightning! So when I heard the first crackle of thunder, I said, "That's it; I'm not going to stand here and get struck by lightning!" (Although I'm sure there were a few people on the set and behind the scenes who thought I deserved it!)

Ellen, who was also directing that day, told the crew guys to pick up their gear so we could finish the day shooting in this old decrepit barn that was on the property. Our fantastic and dedicated crew began packing up their gear in the rain and running across the open field with metal light stands and boom microphones. I grabbed Alex Johnson, the line producer of the day, who had been with the show in its heyday, and told her that there was no way I would continue in this storm.

"I'm going to get in one of the cars and go back to the house—and you'd better get those metal poles out of the crew's hands before they all get struck with lightning, or you'll have so many lawsuits on your hands, you'll be in court the rest of your life!"

She knew I was right. Alex found Ellen and suggested that we pick things up the next day. Ellen agreed and that was the end of that. Everyone got back to the house safely! I've always believed in safety first! Especially when "my crew" is in jeopardy! I genuinely loved those kids—even the old farts who had been around longer than me!

By this time the budget had gotten so tight that our producers were doubling as editors on the show. It was another way the suits could get two jobs done for the price of one. The editors' greatest task was to cover up in postproduction whatever the crew failed to get in the field. For example, the producers refused to allow the sound department to use wireless mics, because Ellen thought it would take too long to change them out from one performer to the next, so the sound on location was atrocious. The only way to fix the poor sound quality was in editing. Their solution was to play the background music so loud that the dialogue couldn't be heard! That was their personal version of MTV!

There was one senior editor, Tommy Bornkamp, who was taken out of a real control room and given the new job of teaching these young people (who basically took away his job) how to edit the episodes on their office computers. To be a good editor you have to know how to tell the story. Tommy was a wonderful storyteller. The producers who were now editing the shows didn't have his years of experience of good storytelling. All they had the time to do was cut the show together and move on. The art was completely lost to scheduling and lack of postproduction time. Ellen had made it clear to all of the editors that their jobs were hanging by a thread. They could have been replaced with the snap of her finger, so they all cooperated and did whatever she asked. She had that effect on most everyone—except, it appears, on me.

In one of the first episodes shot in Peapack, there was a scene of Jeffrey and Reva at the lovely little bridge on Swan Pond, where they come to the realization that maybe they have a future together. The setting was beautiful. We were shooting just as the sun was setting, so there was that perfect golden light that looks so great when it is caught on tape. The wind was gently blowing through my hair, making it look pretty and sexy, while the slinky silk dress I was wearing billowed gently in the breeze. Jeffrey tells Reva how beautiful she looks in the dress and how much he loves her laugh, "so loud and full of life." This is the first time Jeffrey expresses his true love for Reva, a dramatic moment on the show, because the viewers were having a tough time accepting Jeffrey and Reva as a couple. They were always rooting for Reva and Josh.

Since the producers had no control room on location, they had no way to see the shots they were getting—or not getting. They could see the playback through small monitors, but it was impossible to tell exactly what they were getting. No one could spot a boom in the shot, a bra strap showing, or an outfit that made my ass look bigger than Texas. As a result, our camera operators, who were the very best in the business, were always told to get shots of insects or fish or birds or flapping flags in the wind—anything the editors could cut away to if they didn't get a focused shot of the actor's face or if the lighting was so bad they couldn't use the shot!

Sure enough, once they got to the edit, it turned out they couldn't use most of the video they had shot of us, so not only did they end up drowning out Jeffrey professing his love to Reva with loud music; they had no cutaways of either of us to use in place of the unusable video. Their solution was to use a loooong shot across the pond toward an American flag flapping in the wind!

Yup. You read that right.

During Jeffrey's poetic confession of undying love, viewers

were looking at a flag! There was no reaction shot from Reva, no long, deep look into each other's eyes. Nope. Just a flag.

Thank goodness I wasn't at work when I watched this particular episode, because I was livid. I talked myself off the ledge until I actually thought about what we could all learn from this disaster. Clearly we had embarked on a new era in daytime television—one I dubbed "Guerrilla Theater." I called Ellen's office to make sure she would be around when I came into work the next day because I wanted to get together. Her assistant asked me what the meeting was in reference to. That was a strange question, because she had never asked me that before. I can only surmise they had been expecting my call. I didn't want to take my frustration out on the wrong person, so I told the assistant that I had some technical questions about that day's show. Ellen's assistant told me she had to call me back. When she did, she said that Ellen was happy to meet with me during my lunch hour the following day.

I tried to control myself when I got to the studio, but I couldn't. I am the type of woman who needs answers. I needed to understand what was happening to our show and why. When I got to Ellen's office, she opened the conversation by saying how much she loved the new Reva-Jeffrey story line.

"That's why I'm here," I said. "I'm confused by what you're saying. If it's true that you love their relationship, then please tell me why the biggest moment in their relationship was annihilated!"

Ellen said she had no idea what I was talking about. I blurted out, "Who is the last person to see the show and sign off on it before it airs?" When she very proudly said *she* was the final word, I told her that she should be ashamed of the lack of quality that our audience was being forced to endure and that she ought to lose her job.

Ellen looked at me like I had three heads, and reminded me that I was in no position to comment on the decisions that were being made!

It was the worst fight we ever had. Ellen didn't like confrontation, especially when I was the one doing the confronting. Whenever I'd go to her office, she usually tried to defuse the situation by asking about my children or some other personal aspect of my life to set a different tone before we got started. This time, there was no attempt on either of our parts to pretend about how we really felt.

Another difference was that this time Ellen stood up to me, something she generally didn't do. She was so angry, I really thought she was going to blow a gasket! As I stood in her office listening to her go off, I actually had a vision of her head exploding and popping off her shoulders! I decided it was probably best for both of us if I just left her office before things got out of hand.

When I left her office, I felt pretty good because I'd said what I had to say. I'd laid it all out there and was genuinely relieved to have this off my chest. There was also a brief moment of satisfaction in knowing that I had gotten to her. I wanted Ellen to be fully aware that someone was watching the show who was more than a fan. I cared about every last detail—perhaps to my own detriment. Still, I left her office glad that she knew I was looking over her shoulder.

Looking back, I am not proud of myself for the way I handled things with Ellen that day. That I took pleasure in knowing I'd gotten to her was a pure reflection of how ugly my work life had become. It was ridiculous and awful to feel good about getting a rise out of someone, especially my boss. My intention was to get her to see my point of view on what the show had become, as both an actress and a viewer, but I don't think that was the end result on that particular day.

As I made my way down the fifth-floor hallway, I realized that everyone in the surrounding area had vanished. They had either left the floor or had safely locked themselves inside their offices behind closed doors. There was an eerie sense of calm that lasted only a moment or two before I heard Ellen's door open behind me. She wasn't finished with me yet. She literally chased me down the hallway, yelling at me until I ran down a flight of stairs to my dressing room. I was so mad that I couldn't breathe. I couldn't get over that our beautiful show was being trashed. The show was their product, but it was my career, a career I felt was being irreversibly damaged. It appeared that it was an easy decision to ruin the show under the guise of making it the new and improved *Guiding Light*. The idea was to change the way daytime programming was being made, but it was so poorly executed that it felt intentional—as if they were trying to kill the show.

My heart was racing as Ellen lit into me. She made it very clear that I had no right to come into her office and tell her how to do her job! And she was right. I didn't. I wasn't running the show. She was. And I realized that there was a lot less money available to produce the show now than there had been in the eighties and nineties, and those budget cuts were certainly not her decision. I suppose she was following whatever orders she had been given to the best of her abilities, given the constraints she was being asked to work under.

In hindsight I now know that she was under a lot of pressure to bring the show in as cheaply as possible—and guess what: She was definitely doing what she was asked to do! Cheap was what they wanted and cheap was what they got! At the time, I just thought they brought Ellen in to carry out a younger, edgier vision. I really didn't understand what was happening at first, though it didn't take me long to catch on that it was all about money.

I know there are people who think Ellen was a hero, that she kept our show on the air two years longer than it would have lasted otherwise. Keeping the show going meant a steady paycheck for lots of people for another year or two.

Knowing now how bad the show ended up being, I wish the suits hadn't kept it on the air those two extra years. I do hope our viewers were happy to have their beloved show for whatever extra time they could get, but as an actor, I found it was nearly impossible for me to leave the studio with my head held high. It got to the point where it became embarrassing. I'd go to industry functions where actors or directors from other shows would comment on how awful our show had become. I wasn't hurt. There was no secret about how I felt about our declining production values, and it was always helpful for me to hear concern from other people outside our show. Some of that concern stemmed from the fact that several executive producers from other shows were closely monitoring Ellen and her money-saving tactics. If they succeeded on our show, they were likely to become industry practice. If that happened, every actor on a soap was facing the same dismal environment we were working in. In many ways I felt like a lab rat, except we weren't looking for a cure for some debilitating disease. No, we were pawns in a study to stop the bleeding—meaning the amount of money it cost to produce a show like ours. There was no right or wrong answer to offer whenever I spoke to people from other shows, so I'd simply accept their concern and say something to the effect that perhaps, in time, things would work out.

Ironically, things got a little better after my blowout with Ellen. The music and lighting greatly improved. The cameras were pulled back a bit so they weren't getting those extreme close-up shots up our noses anymore! It wasn't because I'd pitched a fit; it was because the audience did. They were rejecting the changes to their beloved show and weren't afraid to let CBS know how they felt. There is tremendous power and strength when the collective voice of our viewers is raised. I loved it. I felt vindicated and validated.

CHAPTER SIXTEEN

The Storm Before the Calm

My husband and I spent countless hours talking about our options. We both agreed that the show had become a hot mess. I no longer felt like I wanted to play Reva. It definitely felt like the time had come to move on.

I didn't have an agent. My last experience with representation back in 1998 hadn't gone so well; I ended up leaving that agency for not having my back. It had definitely been a one-sided deal that left a nasty taste in my mouth. The agency basically collected ten percent of my salary on *Guiding Light* while failing to get me any additional work I could pursue while still working on the soap.

In all honesty, it's very difficult to do other jobs when you're a leading character on daytime television. Guest spots on nighttime shows are cast only about a week before the episode shoots; but contractually, we had to give four to six weeks' notice so they could write the character out for the week you'd be working on another show. So those jobs were basically out. Films were a bit better when it came to advance notice, but they usually took longer and filmed outside of New York, so I would have had to take a leave of absence.

Doing theater in New York was the best option, because I needed the time off only for the rehearsals and then I'd be performing in New York at night and could still do the soap during the day! Of course, that worked best if you had no other life. I had a husband and three kids, whom I wanted to spend time with. So that wasn't such a hot idea for me either.

So the agent's hands were basically tied. But I didn't need an agent just to negotiate a soap opera contract every so often. In the three years that I paid that agency a commission on a job they had nothing to do with my getting, I had maybe *five* auditions for other gigs. It was ridiculous.

That was when I decided to start negotiating my own contracts. Truthfully, I left most of the heavy lifting in the hands of my business manager/lifesaver/friend, Ed Iannicone, and my husband. Together, we negotiated all of my contracts from 1998 to 2009. All of my negotiations on *Guiding Light* were done with a woman named Susan Savage, the lawyer for Procter & Gamble Productions and later TeleNext. Susan is amazingly talented at her job! She knows everything there is to know about negotiating a corporate deal. I warned Ed about Susan before he met with her for the first time; I told him how she would turn on the charm before cutting your throat! Sure enough, Ed called me back after their conversation and went on and on about what a sweet, articulate, funny, warm, and gentle woman Susan was. I broke him out of his love-fest by reminding him why Susan had kept her job for over twenty years: She was a shark!

I adore Susan Savage and to this day we always have wonderful conversations at *Guiding Light* functions and anywhere else we may bump into each other. We usually talk about our children, never "the job"!

I love the thrill of a negotiation; it's like a chess game. I had learned early on from my first agent, Brian Reardon, that when

I went into a negotiation, I had to be willing to walk away from the table if people weren't willing to come to terms with my needs. As he said, you have to have the guts to lose the job! This was an extremely hard lesson to live by, but one that put the ball in my hands. I thank Brian, may he rest in peace, every day for the important lessons he taught me about "the negotiation."

In a standard soap contract, the basic variables are: the length of the contract (usually three years, but sometimes as many as six), the episode fee, and the guaranteed number of episodes you work in each of your negotiated cycles. First-timers usually work on thirteen-week cycles and then graduate to twenty-six-week cycles. Of course, there are some established actors who have achieved enough status to work on fifty-two-week cycles.

The contracts always worked in favor of the producers. At one point, the powers that be were locking up young actors on newer soaps to five- and six-year contracts with only small pay bumps along the way. Don't get me wrong: I understand that a contract is a contract and the actor agreed to the terms. No one forced anyone to sign. But overall, it still seemed unfair.

And, of course, even after an actor signed a contract, the producers always had the option to release him from that contract at the end of his negotiated cycle. So it wasn't unusual for a first-timer to join the show, relocate to New York, sometimes moving an entire family, only to find themselves fired and out of a job thirteen or twenty-six weeks later. (Cough, me and *One Life to Live*, cough.) Every three years, when AFTRA, the television actors' union, renegotiated the standard contract, this was a point of contention. We continually fought for mutuality of contract. What if an actor decided after thirteen weeks that the character wasn't what he or she thought it would be? What if the actor missed his family and wanted to leave? Shouldn't he have the same option to give notice and dissolve the contract? So far, the union has had no luck on this front.

Luckily, my personal experiences with contracts in the thirty years I've been doing daytime television have been pretty good. Not a bad track record, eh? In all my years of negotiating contracts, there was really only one time when things got very hairy. Ed and I had negotiated my last great contract before "the crunch" happened in daytime. It was a tough time for almost everyone. Actors were being asked to take pay cuts when their contracts came up or they were being taken off "contract" status and put on recurring status, which meant they no longer had a guaranteed number of episodes they were paid for per year. I considered it an insult to all the actors who had been on shows for years. After all, they were the true workhorses. Suddenly, they were being given no financial security to speak of.

In May of 2006, I was nearing the end of the first year of my new three-year contract, and, of course, the show had the right to release me at the end of any of my fifty-two-week cycles. I was called into the executive producer's office along with the overseeing producer from Procter & Gamble. They sat there and told me that I was going to have to take a pay cut. My initial thought was to start laughing hysterically, but I thought better of it.

Instead I asked them to tell me why. After listening to their lame reasoning, I said I would be more than happy to discuss a pay cut at the end of my contract, which was in two years, but not now. I wanted only to stand up for myself and have them respect the contracts actors worked so hard to get over the years.

That was when they decided to play dirty.

"Well, if you are unwilling to take a pay cut, we are going to be forced to fire a number of actors on the show. Eight, to be exact," they told me.

Excuse me?

Were they kidding?

Where I come from, a contract is a contract. I thought it was the height of unprofessionalism to come to me in the middle of my term to ask me to take a pay cut. What's the point in negotiating a contract if the terms aren't going to be upheld by both parties?

I wanted to scream and yell and stomp my feet at the absurdity of their actions. I wanted to slap them with a breach-of-contract claim—but I didn't have the fight in me to say those words out loud.

Not to mention, it was kind of hard to comprehend how cutting my salary in half would cover *eight other actors' fees*. I certainly was well paid, but I didn't make *that* much money! And half of my salary wouldn't have meant a thing if the show stayed where it was. This was a no-win situation for everyone.

Unfortunately, other actors had already agreed to take a pay cut as the only way to keep their jobs. Most of those actors were young and in a lower salary bracket than I was. They not only wanted the job—they needed it. Looking back, I think if we had all stood firm and together, we could have avoided being shanghaied, but the executives were smart about how they executed this plan, going to the rookies first and then to the veterans.

I had heard rumblings that Eric Braeden went through the same thing on *The Young and the Restless*, except he decided to walk instead of negotiate. I knew what I had to do. I gave the executives my decision with little hesitation. I said no. I told them I would consider a pay cut at the end of my contract, but would not entertain the thought now or anytime before my contract was up for renewal. It was a very stressful time for me. If they needed my money more than my character, then their only option was to fire me at the end of the fifty-two weeks!

I was pretty sure I knew what their choice would be: to cut me loose. The deadline to give me their decision happened to fall on the same day as the 2006 Daytime Emmys. All day long, I had that terrible feeling one gets when expecting the worst. Even as I got dressed and put on my makeup, I kept thinking that any minute now, they were going to deliver that final blow. I kept waiting for someone to hand me a pink slip, or to tell me that our executive producer wanted to see me in her office. But the day came and went without any notification.

Whew!

I dodged a bullet.

The worst thing, as it turned out, was that the whole time I was just being used as a decoy! The executives were planning all along to take those eight actors off contract so they would have to work at reduced day fees, and with no guarantee for more work. They wanted to use me and my refusal to take a cut in pay as their scapegoat. And that was exactly what happened. Somehow, the story "leaked" that certain actors on the show refused to take a pay cut, so other actors were forced out of their contracts.

"Is it Zimmer?" the press asked, more often than I hoped they would.

It was obvious who it was, but the truth never came out, because the producers feared my response if they actually tried to pin it on me in the press. I posted a statement on my Web site that explained the real story so fans of the show wouldn't be disappointed in me. I also went directly to the actors who were affected and explained my position to them face-to-face so they too would understand that a) I was merely adhering to the terms of my contract, which had been agreed to by both parties, and b) they would have been taken off contract regardless of my decision. Most of the affected actors knew what I was saying was the absolute truth. But to my surprise, there were people who actually believed I was to blame. Some of the message boards and soap press tried to make it a big scandal. Sadly, after the dust settled, even more actors were taken off contract. And, like the others, it had nothing to do with my salary.

The experience left me feeling violated and angry. Throughout the entire situation, I kept hearing the voice of my old agent, Brian Riordan, whispering, "You have to be willing to lose the job." And I was. I was ready to walk rather than give up what was right.

CHAPTER SEVENTEEN

Losing Mom

When I got the word that *Guiding Light* was going off the air, I felt like a huge part of my life was being ripped away from me. I was fired after twenty-six years of dutiful service. It was no different from ending a twenty-six-year relationship. It was the beginning of the worst breakup I ever had—on-screen or off. Unfortunately, it had been dying a slow and painful death, and now someone had wisely pulled the plug while we still had a shred of dignity left. When the suits gave us the final word that fateful day in April 2009, it was as if someone had decided to pull the plug on my life too.

A dark cloud had fallen over me, and I began to carry it everywhere I went. I fell into a depression that I wasn't expecting. I had spent years embracing my lucky and blessed life—but now I could only wrap my arms around the negative.

Acting was never *just* a job for me. It's a job for a lot of actors—a great way to make some money—but that isn't how I saw my career. For twenty-six years, the writers on *Guiding Light* wrote their hearts out not just for you, the fans, but for me, the actress who was lucky enough to bring my character to life five days a week. They challenged me in every way, and I'd like to believe that I always rose to the occasion.

I never played a scene less than what I believed to be one hundred percent.

Not ever.

If I wasn't feeling well, the character didn't suffer.

I never phoned it in. It simply wasn't in my makeup.

My father was a hardworking blue-collar man, while my mother was fully committed to raising her two daughters with no aspiration to be anything other than the best mom she could be to us. It took great fortitude to raise my sister and me. I attribute my work ethic to the excellent examples set by both of my parents. Pleasing my parents was always important to me, but it was really my father's approval I was usually seeking, because my mother unconditionally embraced me and my decisions—especially my choice to become a professional actress. My mom never doubted or tried to sway me from pursuing my career—and that meant the world to me.

On the afternoon of April 8, a week after I was notified of *Guiding Light*'s cancellation, my sister called to tell me that our mother's health had taken a turn for the worse. Over the course of the preceding two years, my mother had suffered a series of undetected strokes as well as the unexpected onset of dementia. She had lost her ability to communicate with words, but oh, boy, she could still communicate with her beautiful blue eyes, which were almost translucent blue. They were starry while mine are more steely. Still, I was blessed with her beautiful blue eyes and will always be grateful for that inheritance.

The last time I'd seen my mother was about three months earlier. She wasn't doing well on that visit, but even though she was hurting, she still looked at all of us with such pride and love. I don't remember a time either one of my parents ever looked at my sister or me with anything but pride. They had set such a fine example of admiration and respect for us.

Mom and I shared so much over the years. Whenever she called, we'd go through all the family news first, but ultimately, the conversation always took a turn toward the show. She'd ask all sorts of questions and offer up her opinion on what story lines she liked and didn't like, hairstyles, hair colors, what she thought about my weight, my clothes, and the other actresses and actors she liked or disliked! Talking to her was always loads of fun, because she had insight and perspective that, well, only a mother can have.

Through the years, my dad humored my mom by watching our show as well, but it was my mom who was the true diehard. It was hysterical to get her all riled up about future story lines. Most of the time she didn't want to know the inside scoop because she wanted to be surprised along with the rest of the viewers. She loved to let the show unfold day by day, even if she had an inkling of where things might be headed.

Mom kept up with all the daytime television industry magazines too. Unfortunately, she had a tendency to believe everything she read. I told her that the stories were usually sensationalized to grab a buyer with headlines that had nothing to do with the actual story. Sometimes she believed me and other times I think she wanted to believe them—if for no other reason than that it made life just a little more fun for her.

A perfect example was a story that ran in 1990 about me leaving the show. *Star* magazine ran a front-page headline that read, "Zimmer walks away from million-dollar contract!"

I wish!

But I was never offered a million-dollar contract—ever. Who knows, perhaps Susan Lucci was making that kind of money in 1990! But it wasn't long before my mom and dad called to ask why I would walk away from a million bucks. I told them the show didn't offer me a million-dollar contract, and if they had, I certainly would have had to rethink my decision to leave. They had a hard time with that, because in my parents' hearts, I was worth *ten* million! They couldn't understand why the show wasn't ponying up whatever it would take to keep me.

My mother was my number one fan. For the first seven years I was on *Guiding Light*, I shot scenes almost every day, which meant she could see me on her television five days a week. Still, it was never enough for my mom. Whenever the show focused on other characters for a change, she got ridiculously ticked off.

"Why have they put you on the back burner? Why isn't the story about Reva?" she'd ask me over the phone.

Talk about a spoiled fan! But I loved her for it.

Anyway, when my sister phoned about my mother's condition, she said that the doctors thought it was time to move her from her room in the assisted-living facility into hospice care. I knew that hospice meant her time with us was short.

"Kim, there's more." My sister paused. I knew it couldn't be good news.

"Her doctors don't expect Mom to make it through the night."

Hold on. I wasn't especially surprised by my sister's call, but I was not emotionally ready to hear that! A small part of me had been clinging to the hope that somehow, some way, my mom would miraculously pull herself through and come back to us. I foolishly hoped there would eventually be some miracle pill she would be able to take that would get her up and out of her wheelchair. She'd be able to talk and laugh again, take trips to the mall, and shop at our favorite flea markets. I would have given anything to get the chance to watch her dance with my dad one last time! They would have been married sixty-eight years in August of 2009.

I told my sister that I would be on the earliest possible flight to Michigan! It wasn't going to be easy, because I was scheduled to work almost every day on *Guiding Light* over the course of the next two weeks. There was no doubt that my absence was going to wreak havoc with rescheduling and post-taping my scenes, but I didn't care. I needed to get to my mother. I wanted to be by her side.

After I hung up with my sister, I immediately called the studio and asked to speak to whichever producer was available. Jan Conklin (the same woman who waited for me in the rain the day we got our notice of cancellation) picked up my call. I explained that my mother was very sick and that I needed to fly to Michigan ASAP! I wasn't asking for permission. I just said, "This is what I need to do."

Jan said, "By all means, Kim. Don't worry about anything here. Just go and be with your family!"

It is that level of kindness that a person remembers during these hard times in our lives. In my time of need, I was pleasantly reminded that the cast and crew were my family too. As I frantically called around trying to put a plan together, they supported me every step of the way. There were many moments in my years on the show when I witnessed a great deal of compassion and love. This, by far, was the most important to me.

Because of the overwhelming love and support of the cast and crew, I was able to jump on a flight within two hours of receiving my sister's call. My good fortune ran out when I ended up missing my connecting flight from Detroit to Traverse City. Panic swept over me when I learned it was the last flight to Traverse City for the night. I was left with two options: rent a car and drive five hours north by myself, late at night, or try to sleep and catch the first flight out in the morning. Hearing what a nervous wreck I was over the phone, my sister insisted I not even think of driving the rest of the way, and get on the first plane out in the morning. Luckily, I made it to Bellaire, Michigan, by nine thirty a.m. and was with my family by ten. My mother peacefully slipped away that evening surrounded by her family.

My beautiful mother—my champion and biggest fan—was gone. I know deep in my heart that she waited for me to come back to be with her! I don't know what I would have done if I hadn't gotten to tell her how much I loved her and thank her for the wonderful life she'd provided me.

There is always some level of regret in death. Mine was that I didn't spend enough time with my mom and dad during their later years. I was always working. And when I did have some time off, I usually chose to spend it with my husband and children. It was a small comfort to know that at the very least they were able to stay connected with me by watching *Guiding Light* every day. I truly don't believe they ever missed a single episode in all my years on the show. Even if they went out for the day, they taped it on the brand-new VCR they finally bought so they could record the show and watch later.

A few years ago, my parents sent me boxes of VHS tapes of all of the episodes they'd recorded. Someday I'll have to transfer them to DVDs to preserve their value to me. Or maybe I'll just make boxed sets to give to the fans! (Hey, I would if I could, but of course, that isn't a real option. You need to appeal to the folks at Procter & Gamble for that!)

It's easy to look back and say, "I wish," "I should have," "I could have," but what is the point in doing that to yourself when you cannot change the outcome? I know there's a natural cycle in life, but there will always be regret for my not having spent more time with my parents. Sometimes I wondered how different my life would have been if I'd had the ability to hop in the car and drive a few miles up the road to see my parents or have my children see their grandparents. Because of my career, I had no choice but to live in the vicinity of the studio where I worked, whether New York or Los Angeles. That meant I was always going to be a plane ride away from a family visit. Unfortunately, those didn't happen as often as I wanted them to. I was lucky to get back to Michigan twice a year. In my heart, I wanted to be more present for my mom and dad, but the realities of my career simply didn't allow for that. And now that my mom was gone, I would never have the chance to make those visits with her again. What I learned from this is how precious family really is to me and how important it is to make those visits happen. I see my dad more today because I realize just how short life can be, and I don't want to let another opportunity pass us by.

It was incredibly hard for me to recover after my mom's passing. Just when I wanted to do nothing but mourn in peace with my family, I realized I had to be in New Orleans the following week for a Super Soap fan event I had committed to six months earlier. I didn't want to go, and the organizer, Mike Gold, understood my circumstances and was kind enough to leave it up to me as to whether I would attend or not. After giving it some sincere thought, I decided to go, because I knew the fans would want answers as to why *Guiding Light* had been canceled. I thought talking about it would actually make me feel better about everything, and I was more than willing to be the goodwill ambassador for the show, even if I didn't feel good about what had happened.

I'm really glad I chose to go, because I was surrounded by so much love and support from fellow actors from other CBS shows as well as the fans. There was great comfort in knowing hundreds of people who felt the same way I did after hearing the news that our beloved show had been canceled would be gathered together.

Before I left for New Orleans, I had made a conscious decision that I wouldn't subject our fans to my mourning for my mother, because that was something I wanted to do in private. They were in mourning for *Guiding Light*, and in a way, so was I. That connection was enough to bring us all together without the added sadness I felt about losing my mother too. I had no idea how I was supposed to console three hundred or so fans, but I knew they were looking to me to offer them some comfort.

At one point during the event, I found myself walking into the audience to embrace a woman who was so bereft that she was shaking and crying.

"Why are they doing this to us?" she asked me. "You're my family. What are we supposed to do now?" This beautiful woman was heartbroken! In some respects, I totally sympathized with her; like so many fans, she had committed an hour a day for who knows how many years to watching *Guiding Light.* At the same time, there was a part of me that wanted to give her a shake and yell, *Get a life!* I had just buried my mother and this woman was sobbing uncontrollably over what is, after all, just a *television show.*

But then I was reminded through her tears that our show had meant so much to so many people. If I'd wanted to shake her a minute before, all I could think of then was to embrace her and support her in her time of sorrow. I looked into her eyes and told her to enjoy that extra hour of her day. She'd now have the time to take a walk, have lunch with friends, or go to a movie with her son. I wanted her to take that time and make it matter.

After hearing what I had to say, she relaxed a bit in my arms. I found a folding chair to sit her back down on. In that moment, I felt like Mother Teresa! The experience with that woman was just the beginning of the outpouring of love, support, and concern from our fans across the country. I may have been feeling down, but the fans were always there to pick me back up at every turn. We were friends and, for some, even family.

Just like my parents, these fans had kept tabs on me through *Guiding Light.* They got to see my hairstyles change, my weight fluctuate, and even watch my second and third pregnancies on the show, since the writers found a way to make Reva pregnant both times. It was great not to have to hide my pregnancies, because it meant my parents could enjoy the progress along the way, if only on television.

I had just found out I was pregnant with my son Max when we were scheduled to shoot Josh and Reva's first wedding. The wedding took place on location at a beautiful property in the Catskill Mountains of New York. It was a weeklong shoot, which made the entire event feel like a real wedding on- and offscreen. It was just like a real-life family wedding. We'd work all day, and then, at night, when we were done shooting, we all ate together and played poker and had a great time. We laughed and giggled all night long. Some of those who had a little too much to drink the night before would show up hungover in the morning, having to go to the wedding all over again. Thank God I was pregnant so my fun was limited!

Larry Gates, the actor who played H. B. Lewis, had a little incontinence issue at this point. If he laughed, he'd pee. Being pregnant for the second time, I could relate to his predicament. The two of us had several scenes together, as he was the father of the groom (and, of course, my ex-husband!).

Larry and I had one particular scene together where we shared a dance in a beautiful field. Thank goodness I was wearing a big antebellum bridal gown, because I was peeing all throughout our dance. I had to take off my underwear because it was so hot while we were filming, and I had to urinate with such frequency, it just didn't make sense to keep pulling up that big ol' dress just to pull down my drawers. It got to the point where I'd find a quiet, semiprivate place to stand off to the side of the field and just go.

I made the mistake of telling Larry what I was doing. Whenever he'd spot me standing off to the side, he'd point over at me and announce to the rest of the crew that I was going to the bathroom. The only flaw in his plan was that every time he did, he'd begin to laugh and end up peeing too. Whenever something funny happened on the set, we ended up doing what I called the "pee-pee" dance, a special dance we made up so we could avoid urinating in our clothes!

Many years later, Reva was expecting a late-in-life baby. Everyone was excited about Josh and Reva having another baby together. Reva was experiencing all of the classic symptoms of pregnancy, which was thrilling and scary at the same time. After all, Reva was up there in years when this story line came around. When she finally went to the doctor for her first prenatal appointment, Reva was told she wasn't pregnant—she was in the first stages of menopause.

Reva, being a vibrant woman who oozed sexuality, was devastated by the news. She was so freaked out by the notion that she was going through "the change" that she ended up pushing Josh right out of her life. Even though she told him it was because he wasn't man enough for her, the real reason was the complete opposite. She felt like she was no longer enough of a woman for him.

The significance of this story line for me was that I too was going through menopause, so I knew exactly how Reva felt. My family and friends watched as I endured all of the classic symptoms of someone going through menopause—while, yes, going through it! Unlike Reva's, my marriage was rock-solid even though I was in the midst of these changes to my body—so much so that I could gain weight without my wonderful husband ever calling me out on it. What a guy, huh?

I figured that if I was going through the change, then I ought to bring all I had to Reva as she experienced it too. I wanted her to have hot flashes at cocktail parties and forget where she put her car keys, just like me.

I remember when my mom went through menopause, she became super-duper hypersensitive. She snapped over the smallest things. My dad reassured me that she was just going through a change in life—that she would be fine. And she was. Once she got through it, she was my mom again. Other than her short fuse, she didn't have a lot of the other symptoms, so I thought I'd have an easy go of it.

Yeah, right!

My mom was still lucid when I began the early stages of menopause, so luckily, I was able to talk to her about our mutual experiences. I told her that I felt sad about not being able to have any more babies. I mean, it was the farthest thing from my mind, but now even if I wanted one, it was no longer an option. Something about that somehow made me feel like less of a woman. I now understand what Suzanne Somers meant when she declared in her book *Ageless* that she loves having her period!

My nearly six years of enduring menopause took a real toll on me physically and emotionally. Menopause wasn't kind. And it was worse because I had let myself go in so many ways. I had gained weight and had gotten very out of shape.

My first indication that I was premenopausal was a change in my periods. I started bleeding in clumps instead of a regular flow. I had my last normal period back in 2004, around the time my daughter, Rachel, graduated from college.

And then the hot flashes arrived.

Yeah, the unexpected, uncontrollable, unwanted, seem-to-show-up-at-the-worst-possible-time hot flashes. They were terribly embarrassing. I'd be in the middle of a scene and would begin to sweat profusely. My body temperature ran somewhere around boiling most of the time—especially under the hot lights on the set. Whenever we'd break, I'd ask my makeup artist if she could see the sweat pouring from my body.

"No!" she'd say. "You're glowing. You look beautiful!" Of course, I knew she was lying. I wanted to die of embarrassment.

My husband couldn't take the heat my body radiated in bed.

Now, stop!

I know what you're thinking, but I am not talking about wild sex.

No. Sadly, I am referring to the furnace he slept next to every night until he couldn't take it anymore.

"Sleeping next to you is like sleeping in a sauna!" he declared.

I had no idea what he was talking about. I insisted the windows be open and the covers remain off all night long . . . only to pull the covers back up and close the windows again. It got so bad, A.C. finally moved into another bedroom so he could get a decent night's sleep. I would have loved to have my man next to me in bed when I awoke every morning, but I also understood that my ailment wasn't his.

Another lovely side effect of menopause was my unexpected weight gain. It was like someone blew up a balloon inside my entire body. Viewers noticed my ever-growing physique, but no one knew the reason why, so there were all kinds of stories and speculations about why I was "letting myself go."

To make matters worse, I didn't have the motivation or energy to do anything about it. I wanted to hit the gym, but I couldn't seem to drag my ass there. I am a pretty energetic woman who always took great pride in the way I looked. The more I packed on the pounds, the worse I felt about myself, and still, I refused to do a damn thing about it. I spent almost six years believing I could kick menopause in the butt while it was slowly spreading mine!

My weight gain had become so noticeable that I was even offered a deal with Nutrisystem, which was worth a lot of money.

There was a catch. They wanted to tie the new campaign in to a story on the show where Reva thought she was too heavy!

Oh, no, they didn't!

Reva would never have admitted to anyone that she was fat! I didn't think it was right for the character, so I turned it down.

On the other hand . . . I'd been successful with Nutrisystem after the birth of Jake. I certainly would have been open to the offer if I could have done the ads as Kim Zimmer. But I didn't want to do a "fat story" with Reva!

I probably burned that bridge, but if I had known then what I know now, I would have said, "Yes!" as quickly as the offer came in. What the hell, right? And just in case you're still interested, Nutrisystem, I'm available!

With the onset of menopause, my energy was simply zapped. And that's not the only thing that was shot. Nope. My patience was gone too. I didn't have patience for anything, but most of all for people who didn't get what I was going through. When I finally went to the gynecologist to get things checked, he said that I was perimenopausal. He immediately suggested putting me on estrogen to balance out my hormones, but I declined. I didn't think I needed medication to get me through. I didn't want to take hormones or swallow pills to help regulate my system. Except for the prenatal vitamins I'd had to down during each of my pregnancies, I hate taking pills! They make me sick to my stomach. If my health depended on taking pills, it wouldn't get done. I couldn't take birth control pills, and I don't even take aspirin when I have a headache!

I have a girlfriend in Montclair who was going through menopause at the same time as me. One day I showed up at her house and saw her putting fifteen or twenty pills into a little case she carried around with her. I have to admit, she looked and felt great, but I didn't want to be "that" woman. Who has the time to monitor that much medication? Besides, I thought I could just wing it and get through the hot flashes and other changes I was going through.

Boy, oh, boy, did I have that all wrong! I should have called an endocrinologist, who would have quickly helped me regulate my thyroid and my weight. I was so stubborn in my decision not to help my body as it went through its changes. To be fair, who knew this condition would last for close to six years? I suppose if someone would have shared that possibility with me, I might have made a different decision.

I don't know if I was in denial or what, but I didn't handle it well. What was I thinking, trying to dig my heels in against Mother Nature? Drawing a line in the sand over my contract is one thing, but trying to stop the tide or turn back the clock is something else. Battling nature is a fool's game. There's only so much you can do about the natural progression of life and aging, and I wasn't open to any of the options that were placed in front of me. My poor husband would gingerly remind me that there were options available, pills I could take to feel better. He even suggested I try bioidentical hormone replacement therapy.

What man even knows about that?

Oh, right, a caring and tuned-in man married to a woman going through menopause!

Menopause is rough—at least, it was for me and so many other people I know who've been through it. I have a very dear friend, a well-known actor, who blames the demise of his marriage on his wife going through menopause. He told me many stories of times she was flipping out and he would hold her in his arms and rock her like a baby, assuring her that they could get through this, reminding her of what her doctors had told her: that her unsettling reactions were just symptoms and would pass. Her response was to lash out, tell him she hated him and didn't want to be married anymore. Undaunted, he assured her that those feelings would pass, that she would love him again. Although I don't think he ever gave up hope, ultimately she gave up on the marriage. She went haywire and never bounced back.

I thought the menopause story line was important to share with our viewers. As bad as I felt myself, I knew there were many women out there who had it much worse. Even though I didn't push A.C. out of my life like Reva did to poor Josh, he and the rest of my family surely suffered through the various stages of menopause with me—every day for years.

Unfortunately, the menopause story on *Guiding Light* never took off. I am not sure why the writers abandoned the idea, but I regret that they did. So many women who watched the show would have been able to relate to the ups and downs of this condition that every woman goes through but few talk about.

When I was going through the change, I often thought about Reva. She was such a survivor. She would have done whatever it took to put a stop to her discomfort. She wasn't one to tolerate something she didn't want in her life. No, she'd just jump off a bridge and swim to an island, where she would meet a handsome prince—but wait. Even if she did, she wasn't going to be in the mood to make love once she got there so that would never have worked! No, Reva would have looked menopause square in the eye and said, "You're not going to kick me when I'm down!"

Unfortunately, I didn't have her resolve.

I was wallowing in my self-pity and anger about life as a more "mature" woman *and* at the deterioration of the show I loved and adored.

And if that wasn't enough to swallow, I had to shop for a dress to attend what would officially be my last Daytime Emmy award show—at least as the actress who played Reva. I began to panic as I also realized there were going to be potential future employers staring at me, asking themselves if they wanted me for *their* show. I was forty pounds overweight, a few months away from being unemployed, and genuinely worried. I decided on a one-shoulder black dress with big white fluffy flowers across the bosom. At the time I thought the dress looked good and the black was very slimming. Little did I know that it really made me look more like Shamu the killer whale!

I had to catch a five fifteen a.m. flight to Los Angeles so I could be in California with enough time to attend a rehearsal for the show. I was tired and a little ragged as I boarded the plane.

I was very sad, thinking this might be my last Emmy awards ever. Fortunately, TeleNext was footing the bill to fly the entire cast, several producers, writers, and members of the production staff to Los Angeles for the three-minute *Guiding Light* tribute planned for the show. Yep, *three* minutes. After seventy-two years of daytime excellence and countless Emmy awards to the show's name, that was all the time they were giving us. Oh, well, I guess it's better than a smack on the ass and a passing thank-you for the years of service.

During the dress rehearsal, we were told that all of the actors would be asked to come up on the stage after a short video honoring the show. The producers had no idea where anyone should stand, because they didn't know the history of the characters, who had been on the show the longest, or who should be standing in the front. Fortunately, someone finally stepped in to help the segment come together. Personally, I thought it would have been cool if, as part of our tribute, they would turn up the lights in the theater and ask anyone who had anything to do with *Guiding Light*, in front of or behind the camera, to please stand up! I can guarantee that three-quarters of the audience would have been on their feet! Now, *that* would have shown the impact that *Guiding Light* had on the industry.

The next day, during the actual show, we all left our seats in the theater and were led out to a back alley, where we waited to be ushered back into the building and onstage. They explained that there wasn't enough room for the entire cast backstage, so we had to wait outside in the burning sun with no protection. All of the actresses' hair and makeup went to hell while we waited around before being escorted back inside. I felt like we were a large group of cows being herded back to the pasture as we got into our positions. The stage manager was yelling at us to pay attention because this was "our" tribute.

Here I was, standing backstage at the Daytime Entertainment Emmy Awards with the most wonderful cast in daytime television as we were about to be honored and applauded by our peers.

And all I could think was "Moo."

It turned out that the show was running long, so the Emmy producers made an executive decision to shorten our clip. Yup. They had run out of time for our tribute. The entire segment ran less than five minutes. First the amazing and talented Betty White gave a warm and heartfelt speech, which took the first two and a half minutes. In her monologue, she joked that she had been a fan of the show since it first went on the air in 1776!

The clip ran about a minute and a half. The remaining thirty seconds was given to a shot of all of us standing onstage like a collection of bobble-heads. The camera was supposed to pan across the entire group while we waved and bowed, as the director had instructed us to do. After they had panned about three-quarters of the way across the stage, I noticed they had cut away from our group shot and gone to a commercial. I hoped they would give us just a little more time to soak it all in, even raised my thumbs to the cameras and said, "Keep it live," so they wouldn't cut away. But in a flash we were gone. My heart was broken. After seventy-two years on the air, those thirty seconds onstage comprised our entire tribute.

To be honest, the whole experience was *weird*. I looked out at the people in the audience giving us a standing ovation, and I could sense all of the actors looking up at us thinking, *Poor them*, and *Please don't let this happen to us next year!* and of course, *Check out all of those actors who are now unemployed and looking for work. I hope they're not gunning for my job!* It was strained on so many levels.

Meanwhile, *Sesame Street* was also honored that night. They were given nearly eleven minutes honoring their thirtieth year of programming—twice the time we were allotted. It was a bitter-sweet evening, one that I'll never forget, but I wish it had been a little different. I felt like *Guiding Light* was deserving of so much more than the time we had been given. It was so emotional for me, because I loved the show as both an actress and as a fan. I knew in my heart that the fans were going to be as disappointed as I was, and it wasn't the way I thought our show should be ushered out.

When I think about shooting the very last episode of *Guiding Light*, I still get a big ol' lump in my throat. The producers set up the day so that every actor under contract had one last scene to play and every producer got to produce a piece of the last show. Every director got to direct a scene; every crew member from the studio in New York and the house out in Peapack got to be a part of the crew. Everyone who had anything to do with the production of the show got to do something.

As each scene was completed, a producer with a bullhorn would announce the names of everyone involved and how long they'd been with the show—whether three weeks or twenty-five years. Every single person's name was announced, regardless of how long he or she had been with the show, in appreciation of their time, effort, and contribution.

The producers hired a big bus to chauffeur the cast and crew around to each individual scene being shot so we could all watch one another's last day of filming *Guiding Light*. The experience was so overwhelming and fun, but mostly the day was full of long hugs and lots of tears!

I feel so honored to have shared my last scene with Robert Newman and to have uttered the very last word spoken on *Guiding Light*: "Always." *Always* was the catchword of Josh and Reva's long and tumultuous relationship; it summed up in one word both the relationship of Josh and Reva and the relationship of *Guiding Light* and its seventy-two years of fans.

CHAPTER EIGHTEEN

The Show Must Go On

osing your job after more than twenty-five years of loyal service is a tough pill to swallow. It doesn't matter where you work, on a soap or at a bank. When someone hands you that pink slip and says, "You're done," it hurts. For me, I had no idea whether I would ever work again. Acting is all I ever wanted to do and now the rug had been pulled out from under my feet. There wasn't going to be an opportunity to come back someday, like I had in the past when I left the show, since there would no longer be a show. I wasn't alone in feeling hurt by this prospect, because, let's face it, it had been a steady gig for a whole lot of us.

The truth is, I had been contemplating leaving the show when my contract was up in June. When the show was canceled in April, there was a strange sense of relief that someone else had made the difficult decision for me. Of course, once the show was no longer an option, it was the only job I could imagine ever having. It's human nature to want the things we can't have and to let go of the things we sometimes take for granted. When I considered leaving *Guiding Light*, my hesitation was never about getting work. I was sure that doors would fly open and opportunities and offers would be plentiful. A few weeks after hearing the news of the show's demise, I had been offered a television movie with Annie Potts and Drew Seeley that was scheduled to shoot in Vancouver in June. These types of roles came along from time to time. They weren't hard work; the pay wasn't even great; but it was an outside gig, and I believed that these types of roles would keep coming, so I didn't think I had anything to worry about when it came time to securing more work.

I dreamed of doing regional theater, creating a cabaret show, and transitioning into something else in television. I wasn't especially interested in doing another soap, but I wanted to work and was willing to consider most anything that came my way.

I called Marnie Sparer, a well-known and highly respected agent who worked with many actors from our show, to seek her advice on what I should do next. I had met Marnie numerous times over the years and she always told me that when the day came that I decided to seek representation, she wanted the first crack. Well, the day had come. After years of steering my own ship, I was not only willing but eager to hand this responsibility off to someone else who had connections, ideas, and insight into what would be best for me and the future.

"We don't want you to look at another soap. We want you to have the freedom to do whatever comes along, whether it's an indie film or a pilot for a nighttime show."

I thought that advice was solid. I seriously thought that with my experience, I wouldn't have a problem getting another job.

I began doing research on a couple of regional theaters I knew would be happy to book me, but they already had their upcoming summer/fall seasons planned out and none were doing shows that I was right for, so that door closed before I could even crack it open.

I spent the last months of shooting *Guiding Light* watching the younger actors on our show get offers right away, yet no offers were coming in for me. Gina Tognoni went back to *One Life to Live*, Danny Cosgrove was offered a role on *As the World Turns*, and Marcy Rylan moved to *The Young and the Restless*. In all fairness, there are more roles out there for younger actors, so it made sense that they immediately got re-cast on other shows. I knew they had their whole lives ahead of them, with families to support, and I was genuinely happy to see them gainfully employed.

Playing Reva Shayne was so much more than just a job and a paycheck. It was the role of a lifetime. And they say there are no good parts for older actresses! The role had taken me from being a princess on a royal island to living with the Amish to dying three times. I'd been a ghost, a clone, and even a time traveler. And Reva was always in love. Why, just as our show was winding down, a menopausal Reva Shayne, while battling cancer, gave birth to a miracle baby.

There aren't a lot of places left to go as an actress when you've spent so many years playing such a rich part. The only thing I could possibly think of was all the great ladies of Shakespeare. I wondered if I could go back to my stage roots and explore the plays of Eugene O'Neill, Tennessee Williams, and Shakespeare, but those roles are few and far between.

As time passed and as the show was coming to its end, I was furious with Ellen Wheeler, whom I blamed for ruining the show. I was angry that I couldn't get another job right away. I was beating myself up thinking my career was over. And, ultimately, I was mad that because of my years of anger, I was now being forced to confront it as part of my punishment for receiving the DUI.

When I was arrested for drunk driving, I thought it was ridiculous that I had allowed myself to get into that situation in the first place. But driving drunk is no laughing matter. I came to feel I was very lucky that my "higher power" saw fit to pull me over before something tragic happened to me or, God forbid, to someone else.

I thought long and hard about whether or not I should discuss this part of my life in my book. I decided that if by talking about my experiences I could reach out and make just one person think twice before getting behind the wheel of a car after drinking, then my humiliating, embarrassing, and expensive experience will have been worth it. Besides, if I am sharing my life here with you, I can't cherry-pick the good from the bad. I want to give you the whole picture so you know I am human, I am fallible, and I sometimes make mistakes.

As part of my penalty, I was ordered by the court to pay a large fee in lieu of community service. I was also required to attend thirty-eight hours of DUI class and thirty-two Alcoholics Anonymous meetings, and submit to a suspension of my driving privileges for six months. After the six months, my driving privileges would remain on probation for three additional years. And remember, all of this was for a first offense on an otherwise clean driving record.

It wasn't until I started attending my court-ordered AA meetings that I realized there was a lot in my life that needed to be put into perspective.

While I never gave it much thought over the years, there have been moments of clarity in which I have questioned my drinking, past, present, and future.

Am I an alcoholic?

No.

Was I using alcohol to self-medicate and numb the anger I was harboring during my last years on *Guiding Light* and afterward?

Yup.

Have I learned a valuable lesson that "actions have consequences"?

You bet!

Getting busted was a wake-up call for me. That evening in and of itself was enough to convince me that I never wanted to experience anything like it again!

In order to understand my personal relationship with alcohol, I began thinking about my history of drinking. My parents were social drinkers; they had a circle of friends they partied with, but as a family I never remember them having wine with dinner or having a "before-dinner cocktail." My dad wasn't much of a drinker: maybe a little Asti Spumante on holidays and maybe a Manhattan from time to time. My mom loved her Budweiser. On rare occasions I'd see her all dressed up for a party with a martini in hand like she'd just stepped off the cover of *Life* magazine. But I never remember seeing either one of them overserved!

My parents started letting me take sips of their wine or bottle of beer when I was around eleven or twelve years old. The first time I can ever recall getting drunk was in high school. We used to have parties called "keggers," which were mostly beer parties.

I would sometimes drink too much and end up throwing up all night long—especially when I made the mistake of mixing beer with cherry vodka. I'd say I was more of a party girl than an alcoholic. But I will admit that I do relate alcohol to partying and having a good time.

I started my heaviest drinking during my last five years on *Guiding Light*. Let me be clear: Heavy for me was three glasses of wine. You see, *Guiding Light* had become such a negative place for me to be. I was absolutely miserable at work. It wasn't challenging for me anymore. I was able to get away with my drinking and behavior because my job had become routine. I was ready to explore and find passion somewhere else. My liquid lunches made going back to work in the afternoons tolerable and made it easy for me to make fun of the material, which had become weak and often absurd. Me drunk meant a fun afternoon for everyone else. Whenever I'd cop an "I don't need this shit" attitude, you can bet the guys on the crew and the other actors all knew I had been to Jake's Saloon for lunch.

Even if I didn't go to Jake's, I usually ended up pouring myself a glass of wine from my dressing room fridge. I called it my "nooner." It gave me a boost in my confidence, a term I use loosely here, to hide my real feelings behind the outward anger. And I didn't even know how angry I really was until the judge on my DUI case ordered me to attend mandatory AA meetings.

I was very nervous to attend my first meeting. It turns out each meeting is unique, in part because of the groups they attract. Some people are there because they've been told by a judge to be there, while others are there as a last resort. Some people are committed to ninety meetings in ninety days, while others are there for the rest of their lives. Some people bounce around from meeting to meeting so they can experience different people with different stories on a regular basis. The important thing is to find a meeting that feels right for you.

My first AA meeting was held right down the street from my home. I fully expected to see at least one person I might know. I wore a baseball cap and dressed in very casual clothes. I wasn't really trying to hide, but I had never been to a meeting before and I didn't know what to expect, so I wasn't looking to attract immediate attention.

I smelled coffee the moment I walked through the door. I was greeted by a woman who was very sweet and welcoming. It happened to be an open-speaker meeting, at which there wasn't going to be any group discussion, only individual sharing. I sat in the back of the room and listened as various people shared their stories. Many people who spoke that day talked about feeling like they wanted to die. Some talked about losing their families, their jobs. Their alcoholism had gotten so bad, they had put themselves in situations to be killed or to kill themselves. The common thread was a level of self-hatred that was so bad that they no longer wanted to live.

Alcohol was the only thing they had left.

It was their only friend.

One woman said that she carried a pint of vodka with her everywhere she went. Instead of putting on her lipstick or freshening up her makeup, she nipped on the bottle. She described the vodka in a way I'll never forget. She said it was like "having a friend with no legs" that she had to carry around with her. "There were plenty of times that bottle carried me home too. I'd wake up the next morning with no idea how I got there," she said.

Her story moved me in ways I wasn't expecting. I thought back to one particular night that I wish I could forget.

After it was announced that *Guiding Light* was being taken off the air, there was a flurry of industry parties honoring the show. I often felt the need to get toasted at these functions to get through the evening and cope with the fact that we were dying a slow and painful death. Well, the night before the 2009 Daytime Emmys, *Soap Opera Digest* had a big bash; they always threw the biggest, best, and most fun parties. Anyway, this was a gathering bringing all of the East and West Coast soaps together, including a lot of people I hadn't seen in some time. There's usually a lot of drinking at these industry events anyway, but that night I got plowed. Truth be told, I wasn't handling my booze like I used to. My tolerance was gone because of the changes in my hormones from menopause. I'm not trying to make excuses here. It's my fault that I got so drunk that I ended up on the floor. I had literally fallen down and couldn't get up. I was lying there laughing hysterically because I felt like a turtle that had flipped over and couldn't get back on its feet.

Thank God my two dear friends Crystal Chappell, who was on *Guiding Light*, and Hillary Bailey Smith, who was on *One Life to Live*, were there to help me. They got me out of there and made sure that no photographers were able to get any pictures of me in that state.

The more I thought about my drinking, the more I began to realize that it had affected my life, whether I was aware of it or not. A few years back, I'd attended Crystal's baby shower in

New York City. It was a really fun evening—where once again I had a little too much to drink. Luckily, I let someone else drive me home that night. I was usually pretty good about not driving if I was intoxicated. Unfortunately, I had a really early call the next morning. I had to be at the studio by seven a.m. I was definitely going to pay the price for my evening of frivolity and fun.

When I got up the next morning, my husband asked if I wanted him to drive me into work, because, although I was no longer intoxicated, he knew I had gotten only four hours of sleep. A.C. was being persistent about driving me, but I refused. He pleaded with me to take the bus that morning, and still, I said no.

"I can do this drive in my sleep!" I said as I raced around trying to get dressed and out the door. I had made the drive so many times that I thought my car had an autopilot that got me to and from the studio. That particular morning was one when I knew I'd need it. Even though I was tired, I thought I was fine to drive.

I got into my car like any other morning. I headed toward Manhattan like I always did, but drove even more carefully. In fact, I was being so overly cautious that I thought I saw someone changing lanes next to me and pulling into my lane. I overreacted to what I thought was happening, which caused me to spin out of control and steer my little red sports car into the highway median. I spun across four lanes of traffic during the morning rush hour and ended up in a dead stop against the cement median. It was one of those moments when I saw my life pass before my eyes. I saw flashes of my life in fast motion. I saw my children, my husband, my parents, and even our dog. When my car eventually stopped, I realized I was okay. It was nothing short of miraculous that I was able to walk away with only a cracked nose and without hurting anyone else. I fully expected to see a scene of devastation behind me. I thought I must have caused a multicar pileup in my wake.

Nope.

Traffic was whizzing by as if nothing had happened at all.

I had a clear spinout.

A man in a Jeep saw my accident and pulled over to see if I was okay. I asked if he saw the car that was changing lanes. He shook his head no. He said there was no one changing lanes—at least, not that he saw.

I must have nodded off and caught myself in that split second before totally falling asleep. When I woke up, I freaked out.

The man told me I was bleeding, and he was kind enough to get me out of there. Neither of us had a cell phone, so he took me to the nearest pay phone so I could call my husband.

All A.C. wanted to know was whether I was okay. He never once said, "I told you not to drive." No, my wonderful husband isn't like that. He never judges me or crucifies me for my mistakes.

While I waited for A.C. to come fetch me, I called the studio to let them know I had been in an accident. I was going to be late for work, which was going to affect everyone on the set. Fortunately, they were able to reorder the day so production wouldn't be held up on my account.

When A.C. showed up, he insisted on taking me to the nearest hospital to have my nose looked at. Thank God there was nothing seriously wrong. I didn't need stitches, which meant there wouldn't be a scar, but I was definitely going to be black-and-blue. The emergency room doctor slapped a Band-Aid across my superficial wound and sent me on my way.

It turned out that I was only an hour and a half late for work that day. My accident became the benchmark that all of the young actors on the show had to live up to. Whenever someone was going to be late, inevitably one of the actors or producers would tell them, "Zimmer still made it to work after totaling her car! What's your excuse?" I have to say I myself was never very sympathetic to or understanding of people who couldn't get to the studio on time. They were blessed to have jobs as actors. For Pete's sake, find a way to make it to work when you're supposed to!

Six months after my DUI, I was asked to surprise a longtime fan of *Guiding Light* who'd been fighting breast cancer for two years. The doctors had stopped her chemotherapy because the cancer had spread throughout her body. Sadly, they gave her two to six months to live. I spent an hour in her home with her, her husband, and their two beautiful daughters. At some point during our time together, when looking at their family photos, I noticed there was a young man in the pictures. I asked who he was and was told it was their son, who had been killed. After I caught my breath, I asked how he had died. One of their daughters softly informed me that a drunk driver had killed him. My heart shattered into a million tiny pieces. I felt a sense of overwhelming guilt come over me for what I had done. I didn't share my story with the family that day, but in that moment, I made a commitment to myself that from then on, moving forward with my life, I was going to do everything in my power to make sure

I learned from my mistake and never, ever allowed it to happen again.

Drunk driving is a crime that touches many people. When people heard what happened, they all too often said, "Oh, that happened to me too," or, "Hey, it could have been me!"

And yes, it could have been them!

The important question is, What are you going to do to make sure it *isn't* you?

I'm not preaching here; I'm just sayin' that there are so many options available instead of getting behind the wheel of a car after drinking. I was fortunate in that the only thing I hurt the night I got popped was my self-esteem. But sadly, so many others won't be as lucky. Remember, drinking and driving is like playing Russian roulette with your life. Are you willing to take that kind of chance just for a fun night out on the town?

Although I attended all of my mandatory AA meetings to meet the requirements for the court, I never went to an actual twelve-step meeting. Those meetings are private and the court only required me to attend open meetings—those anyone who may be having some sort of problem can attend. I've placed my focus on finding other ways to handle my compulsion to drink, and Lord knows, I will never find myself behind the wheel of a car after drinking ever again.

I haven't stopped drinking, because I enjoy my glass of wine with dinner. I know there are people out there who believe they can moderate their drinking when they really can't. I am not one of those people. I made a poor decision to get behind the wheel after having one too many—something I vow to never do again. My family has supported me throughout this entire ordeal. They know how devastated I've been and how very sorry I am that I made that fateful decision.

It has taken me a while to start getting up in the morning with the desire to get out there and hit it. After losing my driver's license and being forced to walk most everywhere, I really started to enjoy it. I was inspired by a neighbor who told me she walks to the grocery store every day, gets the things she needs to prepare dinner that night, and walks home. I started doing that, and then walking to other places too. I walked to my AA meetings, my DUI class, and everywhere else that was within a four-mile radius of my home. And you know what? I began to feel good. Really good. For the first time in several years I feel reconnected to my family, my home, and myself. My life is no longer locked up and tied in knots because of my turmoil at work. I hope to find passion in other areas of my life too. I will always be an actress, but I'd like to find a way to pass along the experiences I've had and maybe even teach a course or two. I'd like to do films, but not if the part takes more than a couple of weeks. After years of working in the fast-paced world of soaps, I simply don't have the patience to sit around and twiddle my thumbs during all the downtime you have while shooting a movie. Working on a soap is the equivalent of a nine-to-five job for actors. After years of steady work, fifty weeks a year, five days a week, I am ready to explore other opportunities and spend more time with my husband, children, and, for the very first time ever, just me. I now find joy in the little things—something I failed to do for so long—too long.

If you are struggling with something in your own life, I hope you will take the time to look inside yourself and evaluate your situation. When we are young, we think we are infallible. Here's the truth: We aren't. We all make mistakes. It's okay to question your actions, because actions always have consequences. It may take you longer to realize those consequences, but they happen.

There was never any good reason for me to self-medicate like I did. I had a great husband, three amazing children, and a wonderful life. A.C. and I were essentially empty nesters getting ready to embark on the next chapter of our fairy-tale life. I had suffered and survived menopause and was ready to take the tiger by its tail.

I had been nominated for an Emmy a total of eleven times over the years and was lucky enough to take that golden statue home four times. I was surrounded by only positive influences, from my parents to my husband. I was one of the most successful actresses on daytime television. So where exactly did the worm turn?

I never realized that all of those times I turned to alcohol for comfort, it was only fueling my already emotional and overly sensitive frame of mind. I made fun of myself for years as I boasted about drinking my lunch so I could come back and finish my day of work in that hellhole. I'd come back from the bar and was suddenly transformed into Tallulah freakin' Bankhead!

"You people don't know nothin'! Lemme tell you how this is gonna work . . ." and so on. I told the sound guys to turn up my mic so everyone could hear me bitch and complain.

What was I thinking?

If I could, I would turn back the clock and maybe would have left the show before it got to that point, where I felt I had to drink to get through my day. But I can't climb into a time machine and change the outcome of those actions. All I can do is learn from them and know that I am fully aware of why I did the things I did. And through the work and help of the people I met in the program, I now understand that drinking wasn't solving my problems—it was creating them.

If you take away anything from this book, I hope it's to learn from my mistakes. I've made some doozies over the years, but I am thankful most weren't as bad as they could have been. Don't beat yourself up over the past. Learn from it, and move on to create a better future.

CHAPTER NINETEEN

So Long, Springfield

Actors are often asked to travel to various areas of the country to promote their show and to cultivate relationships with the affiliate stations that put the show on the air. I made countless trips like this to promote *Guiding Light* over the years. We weren't paid for these events, but there were a few promoters who figured out how to do this type of "show" for profit, where the actors were paid a fee for their time.

When *Guiding Light* was canceled, one of these promoters came up with the idea to do a So Long, Springfield tour. The concept was to give the fans a chance to spend the day with us and to see a side of each actor that otherwise wouldn't be seen on the air. They could ask questions, have us sign autographs, take pictures with us, and be free to mingle without any restrictions. And, of course, it was an opportunity for us to thank our fans for their years of devotion.

The promoter was a fellow named Mike Gold. He researched the areas with the strongest *Guiding Light* demographics and put together the tour. Since we were all disappointed about the cancellation of our show, these gatherings seemed to come at the perfect time to serve as a kind of catharsis for many of us. To be fair, I think the fans needed the connection every bit as much as we did.

I can't tell you the energy that Mike put into these events. When I heard the idea, I thought at first that he was just trying to make a buck. Maybe he was, initially, but I think the So Long, Springfield tour became something more for him. It was amazing to see anywhere from three hundred to three thousand passionate fans show up to hear whatever the heck we had to say. We gathered in a convention hall in whatever city we were in and just chatted for an hour or two. Anytime actors get together with fans in a setting like this it usually ends up being a blast for all involved.

I worked with Mike to organize groups of actors who we thought would be fun for the fans to meet and see interact with one another. Bradley Cole, Robert Newman, Ron Raines, Marcy Rylan, Frank Dicopoulos, Tom Pelphrey, Michael O'Leary, Gina Tognoni, and Grant Aleksander were just a few of the marvelous actors who agreed to come along for the ride. Later we added Danny Cosgrove, Beth Chamberlain, Justin Deas, and Tina Sloan. By the end we involved almost everyone.

The So Long, Springfield tour kicked off in October 2009, after our last show aired. We spent two days in each city, usually a Saturday and a Sunday, doing two shows. It was reminiscent of the old days, when we went out on appearances at malls to greet the fans, and thousands of excited, screaming people showed up just to get a glimpse of their favorite actors. It really makes you feel like a rock star.

The setup was casual. The morning sessions were primarily focused on meet and greets, so we could be hands-on with the people who came to see us. There were no velvet ropes, guest lists, or VIP sections. It was all up close and personal. In the evening, several director's chairs and sometimes a large, comfortable sofa were placed on a stage, where the actors would sip a little wine while reminiscing about the show and our experiences as actors. So many wonderful, intimate, lovely moments came up for us as we remembered the years we spent putting together the best show in daytime television. It was really a chance for the audience to eavesdrop on an intimate conversation among the actors.

Frank Dicopoulos, who played Frank Cooper, the resident cop, was a teddy bear of a man. He never had a bad word to say about anyone or anything. He is a real gung ho company man in every way. When we got to talking onstage, we usually talked about one memorable scene we shared many years ago, when Reva and Frank were having a very intense conversation about a silver SUV he had found wrapped around a tree. Frank had come to question Reva to see if she knew anything about the accident. Reva's line was "That could be Josh's car." And although I got the line right, I delivered it with such intense concern that it cracked me up—and everyone else in the scene. We broke up so badly that they had to yell, "Cut!"—at which point I added, "I loved that car," with more concern for the vehicle than for Josh. And then there was the time Reva was handing a small box containing cuff links to another character on the show. I said, "Josh and I would like you to have these. They're a pair of handcuffs!" Oops. I think they call that a Freudian slip.

Michael O'Leary, who played Dr. Bauer, was by far the funniest man on our show. I always loved doctors and cops on soaps, because their characters would often drive a scene. Doctors in crisis, cops in crisis. Either scenario usually made for great television. Michael was like a character you'd see in one of those movies about soaps, such as *Tootsie* or *Soapdish*, who could never get his line right. He was constantly using the wrong words but was hardly ever aware of his mistakes. We'd all laugh, while Michael wouldn't have the foggiest idea of why we were cracking up. Robert Newman made one of those gaffes that stuck with him for the rest of his time on *Guiding Light*. He was supposed to say, "ten million bucks," but it came out as, "ten million ducks"! No one heard the mistake, so it made it onto the air. After that, no one ever let Robert live it down! The phone lines at CBS lit up with viewers calling in to say how funny it was to hear Robert say that line. "Ten million ducks" became a running gag on the set for years.

Working on a soap opera is like living in a state of heightened reality. There were countless moments when something would happen that would tickle one person, and then the giggles caught on like wildfire, often to the point where we'd have to stop taping. We'd start over, but more times than not, once the actor got to that same line, it was hard for anyone to keep a straight face. You might notice someone's shoulders shaking, another actor biting his or her lip, or no one making eye contact for fear of breaking the scene yet again. The minute one of us made that eye contact, we'd all lose it and crack up. It was like the old episodes of *The Carol Burnett Show*, with Harvey Korman, Tim Conway, Carol Burnett, and Vicki Lawrence all trying to keep it together and failing. These moments on *Guiding Light* were some of my favorite and healthiest memories of being on the set. They were priceless when they happened and are still loads of fun to talk about all these years later.

The So Long, Springfield weekends were a gift—not just to the fans, but for us too. Tears often welled up as I spoke about my favorite moments, and just as often I'd laugh uncontrollably as I listened to others talk about theirs, especially Michael O'Leary and Grant Aleksander, who shared a dressing room forever. They were great buddies, but they were exactly like Felix and Oscar—the Odd Couple. Michael was messy while Grant was a neatnik. Listening to them talk about all the times Grant freaked out when he found Michael's underwear on the floor is nothing short of hysterical!

After our chitchat, the last part of the evening was dedicated to entertainment. This was the part of the program where each of us performed whatever we liked to do. Bradley Cole played his guitar; Adam Reist, one of our directors, played bass; and a pianist rounded out their trio as they jammed for the audience. Robert Newman sang, as did Ron Raines, who I think is God's gift to big voices. Ron always brings down the house!

And me?

Well, anyone who has watched the show over the years knows I love to sing—especially torchy, bluesy cabaret or high-spirited rock. I have done quite a bit of work in nightclubs over the years. I've even sung the national anthem before a New York Giants football game and before a big game between the Chicago Bulls and my home team, the New Jersey Nets. I met Michael Jordan for the first time about a year or so after he joined the NBA, when he invited me to play in one of his celebrity golf tournaments in North Carolina. It turns out that Reva and *Guiding Light* were both very popular in North Carolina, and my participation helped Michael build and elevate the Michael

Jordan Celebrity Golf Classic that benefitted the Ronald Mc-Donald Houses in the area. We adored each other from the start. So when the Chicago Bulls came to New Jersey to play the Nets, Michael tried his best to crack me up while I stood in their arena singing the national anthem. Lucky for me, I was able to get through the song without losing it. He's such a practical joker that I thought for sure he had a shot at getting me to laugh. After I finished, he told one of the guys on the court that he wanted to see me after the game. I was with my son Max, who was no more than two or three years old at the time. When we got to the locker room, there were dozens of people outside waiting to see members of the team—but most were there to see Michael Jordan. I thought it would take forever for him to come over and talk to us, so I actually contemplated leaving. As soon as he came out of the locker room, he told everyone there that he would get to them but had to get to "this lady first," as he pointed to me. Me! I just about died. Michael came over, picked up Max, and was holding him above his head, laughing and cooing at my baby boy. Of course, I was kicking myself that I forgot to bring a camera with me, but it is a moment I will never forget.

I got to sing on *Guiding Light* several times. One of my favorite scenes was when Reva sang "Proud Mary" at the Blue Orchid nightclub. The host of the nightclub was played by Warren Burton, one of the most delightful and funniest men I've had the pleasure to work with. Warren shared his dressing room with an actor who wore "manty panties," nylons designed especially for men. They're mostly used by men who have varicose veins or some other circulatory condition. There's a special place for men to tuck their "package" so they aren't uncomfortable.

On the day we shot this particular scene, Warren came out onto the set with a pair of manty panties wrapped around his head like a turban, with the package part sticking straight up on top making him look like a rooster. (Insert cock joke here!) That prank got our day started on the right foot!

Unfortunately, I almost ended the day by nearly breaking my neck falling off the bar I was dancing on. Two waiters saved me and I just kept doing my best Tina Turner impersonation. Actors picked up glasses as I shimmied and shook my bonbon until I just lost my footing. Luckily, those two waiters and Warren lifted me off the bar and grabbed me before I could fall. You can see the whole thing, because the director never stopped tape.

There's an old saying in our business that you ought to be careful how you treat people on your way up, because you are sure to meet them on the way down. Boy, am I glad I had a good rapport with Warren, or else I would have fallen flat on my ass that day!

Having the chance to show my chops to our fans at each So Long, Springfield event was wonderful. I belted out a couple of favorites, which is always fun for me and, I hope, entertaining for the audience. Afterward, people often asked whether I was going to record a CD or whether I'd consider doing a Christmas album. The answer is that I don't have any plans to record, but I'm certainly open to the idea! So if by chance either Clive Davis or Quincy Jones is reading this book, feel free to give me a call!

Doing fan events was always something I viewed as a perk of the job I was privileged to have for so many years. For me, my work has always been for and about the fans. So I enjoyed doing events where I could meet the people who faithfully watched our show. That is why it meant the world to me to have it all come full circle again with the So Long, Springfield tour.

In late 2009 we also had our last official fan club gathering, organized by Mindi Schulman and Mary Ann Wortendyke, the presidents of the *Guiding Light* fan club. Every October, they put on an event for the fan club members at the Marriott Marquis in New York City. Fans from all over the country took over the biggest ballroom in the hotel at an all-day event that included lunch and then a question-and-answer session. The last fan club event included a surprise appearance by several actors who had previously appeared on *Guiding Light*, which was a special treat for those in attendance. It was certainly fun for me to see so many familiar faces I hadn't seen in years.

It felt like our own personal Barbra Streisand final-farewell tour. We kept saying we were finished, but kept booking these events. As long as the fans still showed up—and believe me, they did—we would all be a part of this wonderful adventure to keep the spirit and memory of the show alive for as long as we could.

Fans of daytime soap operas are a special breed. When a fan stops me for an autograph or just to talk about the show, it's like seeing a relative they haven't seen in years. It's different from any other celebrity encounter, because we're like members of their family. The relationship is intimate and different from, say, a newscaster, who delivers the news but doesn't offer a fantasy getaway like we do. Our fans laugh with us and cry with us; they live through everything our characters are going through. So they feel comfortable coming up to us on the street because we're family.

It's very rare that I've been upset or annoyed by a fan; one of the few times was when I was with my family at Disney World. There was a woman there who I swear believed that Reva Shayne was a part of her Disney experience, like Mickey Mouse or Donald Duck! She proceeded to push my own young children away from me and replace them with her ill-behaved brood so she could take a picture. Had she behaved like a human being and not some freakazoid, I would have agreed to the picture, but because of the way this woman manhandled my children—and to keep A.C. from punching her out—I informed her that I too was on vacation with my family and I was not a Disney character being paid to deal with pushy people like her! I believe she called me a bitch before she chased down and tackled Cinderella next!

When my husband and I traveled abroad, I'd sometimes forget that American soaps are broadcast in countries all over the world. It was always a little jarring to be recognized in a foreign country. One of the sweetest fan encounters I ever had took place on a trip to Italy with A.C. I love Italy. The men are extremely handsome and the women are so beautiful! We were in Alba, in northern Italy, touring old castles and strolling the scenic streets of the city, when we noticed that we were being followed. I heard the group start to laugh and whisper the word *Sentieri*. I didn't pay it much mind until one of them called out, "Reva?" A.C. and I turned around and were shocked to see six beautiful young Italian guys following us. We stopped and tried to chat, but they didn't speak English and unfortunately we didn't speak Italian. But they were fans and so happy to meet Reva from *Sentieri*, which I later learned means "the light" in Italian. Much to my surprise, I was recognized all over Italy. I don't know why I didn't expect it. Chris Bernau, who played Alan Spaulding in the eighties, had always said he vacationed in Italy as often as he could, because he was such a big star there. He said he never had to pay for anything!

Sometimes a fan can become a tremendous asset, because the true diehards know more about me and my work than I could ever remember on my own. Shelli Miller started out as a fan but quickly became so much more. Shelli is funny, witty, and tremendously valuable, as she now maintains my Web site. To do this takes someone special. I met Shelli in 1999, at the time when the Internet was just starting to explode. She asked if I'd be interested in starting a fan site, a place where fans could talk to one another about the show and write to me, and I could leave them special messages in return. We could post pictures and announcements of other projects I was working on and solicit feedback about what songs they'd like to hear me sing, or their favorite Josh and Reva moments. It was the perfect solution for a person like me, who was always terrible at answering fan mail. And the fact that Shelli was offering to run it for me was fantastic. I was a bit computer illiterate, and I was extremely nervous about what I might (or might not) be able to contribute to the site. Fortunately, Shelli talked me down, and we are now the proud owners of www.kimzimmer.net! The people who are regulars on the site are so talented and creative, making their own banners of shots from *Guiding Light* and creating video montages set to music.

I'm so proud of the work that Shelli and a few others have contributed to make the site an interesting and fun place to visit.

Have I enticed you to check it out yet?

I double dog dare ya!

CHAPTER TWENTY

Fate

We all sometimes think about the road not traveled, and as you might expect, I have sometimes wondered what my life would have been like if I'd never been cast as Reva Shayne on *Guiding Light*.

I can't even begin to wrap my brain around how different my life would have been. The minute I start questioning the decisions I made in my career, it doesn't take very long to convince myself that, if given the opportunity, I wouldn't change a thing!

I have had the privilege to be an integral part of the longest-running drama in television broadcast history. I was deeply honored to be a part of so many of the milestone celebrations we had, including the ten thousandth episode, the fifteen thousandth, right up to the very last episode. Reva Shayne is so relevant that she is part of a time capsule the Museum of Television and Radio buried on its property in New York City. If that capsule is dug up five hundred years from today, I'll be right there, still dubbing myself the Slut of Springfield! That thought makes me giddy!

But as the old saying goes, "All good things must come to an end."

Or do they?

Losing a job for reasons that are out of your control is very difficult, especially in today's economy. As if anyone needs things to be even harder, I work in a business that is laser focused on youth and beauty. The reality of ever working again at the age of fifty-five and carrying an extra thirty pounds around is even more daunting.

I was so comfortable in Reva's skin that I rarely questioned my personal self-confidence, with the exception perhaps of those last few years on *Guiding Light*. I *was* Reva Shayne, whether I was a size six or a fourteen! My waist size didn't matter to the fans or to me—not really. Oh, but don't kid yourself, Zimmer. It definitely matters in the job market! I figured I needed to put Jenny Craig on my speed dial ASAP, or find the nearest fat farm so I could lose my excess weight and secretly recover from whatever plastic surgery it would take to put me back in the game.

There I was, fifty-five years young, thinking that I had to reinvent myself if I ever wanted to work again. Going back to my roots onstage was an obvious option. I auditioned for a role at a regional theater in rural Pennsylvania, thinking I nailed it, and I never even got a call saying they were going with someone else. That was a little tough to take, because I was certain the other actors auditioning didn't have my marquee value.

I toyed with making the transition from television to film, but making movies is truly a totally different beast from doing daytime. I didn't think I had the patience to sit around a movie set all day. I am used to the fast pace of doing soaps.

The few auditions for television that I went on were eye-opening. It felt like I was starting all over again. I felt nervous and desperate, which is not a good combination when trying to land a job! It became painfully obvious that I was no longer Kim Zimmer, the four-time Emmy-winning actress; I was now Kim

Zimmer, the unemployed actress. (I have friends who aren't in the business who don't understand why someone with my experience still has to audition at all. I kindly tell them that unless you're Meryl Streep, *everyone* auditions. I love my friends!)

It took a number of terrible auditions before I started to feel comfortable in those casting rooms again. It didn't help to know that there were a lot of talented actresses out of work who were looking for the same jobs I was going after. There isn't a lot to choose from in the forty- to sixty-year-old roles! I think it was Glenn Close who once said that a working actress goes from being the bombshell to playing the mother and ends up as a district attorney. That's all we have to look forward to as we age in our business.

Egad!

One audition I went on was for a guest spot on the now defunct television show *Eastwick*, playing the mother of one of the regulars. (See above!) Okay, no big deal. I can do this, right?

I signed in at my allotted time and went to find a seat in the waiting room. I thought I'd walked into a wax museum of every famous "mom" from eighties television! There were Joanna Kerns, Meredith Baxter-Birney, Marilu Henner, Dee Wallace, Marisa Berenson, and the list went on and on. There were probably twenty of us all vying for this one small role.

When the casting director called my name, I suddenly found myself totally intimidated by my competition. My audition sucked because of it! It has taken me a year or so to find the strength, courage, and self-belief to walk into these auditions with my head held high because I know I'm just as competent to do the job as any of those fine and talented actresses!

But knowing I can play the role isn't enough. The hard part is convincing some casting director who isn't familiar with my body of work that I am the only possible actress to play the part! That's when the process slips right out of your hands. As actors, all we can do is continue to try to do our best, and then we have to leave the rest to fate! Will I ever get the chance to impress Tommy Tune with my tapping skills? Probably not, but I am prepared to take on whatever happens next with renewed optimism!

Much to my surprise, my life has unexpectedly come full circle. After twenty-seven years, I'm back at the show that fired me, which made it possible to audition for Reva Shayne. Yes, I am once again playing Echo DiSavoy on *One Life to Live*.

Fate.

Yes, I'm a believer!

I was riding in a rental-car shuttle in Los Angeles with Frank Valentini, the executive director of *One Life to Live*. We were both in town to attend *Guiding Light*'s last Emmy awards show in 2009. We spent the fifteen-minute ride to the rental-car lot teasing each other about resurrecting the character of Echo Di-Savoy. I never meant our banter to be taken seriously, but then again, why not, right? Frank ended up calling me a year later to ask whether I was ready to come out of retirement yet. I didn't have to think about that answer too long. After all, who can afford to retire these days?

Yes, I was ready!

I went to Frank's office, where he proceeded to offer me the opportunity to work in the genre I love so much, with my old buddies Erika Slezak, Robin Strasser, Jerry verDorn, Hillary B. Smith, and Robert Woods.

"When do I start?" I asked. This is the work I love to do. It's my passion and my calling.

As of the writing of this book, *One Life to Live* is the last soap opera being produced in New York. It is scary and very hard for me to believe that this is what the soap business has come to. For years, soap operas gave New York actors enough work to keep them eligible for their union health benefits, and now we're down to one. In my heart, I want to believe that some new format of the soap opera will be reinvented, and as it was in the beginning, it'll happen in New York City.

After I agreed to resurrect Echo, I have to admit that I felt a bit of "buyer's remorse." You might say I was excited about moving into my "new house" but apprehensive about paying the mortgage. What I mean is that I was going to be jumping back into the routine of daytime television just as I had found the freedom to explore other areas of this crazy business. But the reality of receiving a steady paycheck again and having the opportunity to play Echo won out!

My agent, Marnie, was great. Any other agent would have said, "Take the job!" but she left the decision totally up to me. A.C. felt the same way. My husband is the only person on the planet who knows me well enough to understand my deep desire to work, as well as how much I love working on soap operas! After giving it a lot of thought, I gave Marnie the green light to call up Frank and accept his offer.

Yee-haw! We were once again off to the races!

I knew being back at *One Life to Live* would be different for me, but I suspected it would be in a really wonderful way. It wasn't "my show," the way *Guiding Light* was. No, this show belonged to the people who had been there for twenty and thirty years! I thought it might be a pleasant change if I could fly under the radar there for a while and not have to worry about all the things I used to worry about at *Guiding Light*. All I needed to do was show up for work, take the written page, and make it come to life. For the first time in many years, I could simply focus on what I was there to do: *act*.

So here I am, having so much fun at *One Life to Live*. I'm working on real sets again, elaborately decorated with real flowers, real food, and—wonder of wonders—real ice cubes! (I say this because we were using plastic ice cubes that got washed and reused at *Guiding Light*.) I have space to move around a New York City set again. The lighting is beautiful. Attention is paid to the smallest details.

What hasn't changed is that the action on the set still moves faster than the speed of sound, but that's what gives daytime such a unique energy. It's an adrenaline rush, like opening-night jitters in the theater. But as daytime actors, we get that rush every single time the stage manager counts down: "In five, four, three, two . . . !"

As long as I live, there will always be moments when I think, *This may be my last job!* But until death comes, I hold on to the hope that there's always another gig right around the corner!

So, as I'm thinking about the final period on the last sentence of this memoir, I find myself facedown in a heap at the bottom of Dorian Lord's fireplace wearing a Santa suit and covered in "makeup" dirt and coffee grinds doubling as soot. When the director finally says, "Cut," I linger for an extra beat, looking up into the clean faces of my scene partners, who are stifling their laughter. And all that crosses my mind is that storied old punch line, "What . . . and give up show business?"

I'm just sayin'!

Tune in tomorrow!

EPILOGUE

D amn, tommorow's here, and I so wish it was yesterday! Just as I was putting the final touches on this book, ABC announced that it was officially pulling the plug on two of its mainstay soap operas: *All My Children* and *One Life to Live*!

As the great Yogi Berra said, "It feels like déjà vu all over again!"

At least this time I know it's not the end for me.

I know that if you stay positive and believe in yourself, there is life after soaps—something I wish I had had faith in when *Guiding Light* first went off the air. I suppose I wouldn't have the same outlook today had I not gone through my mourning period back then. Still, it's sad to think that the daytime soaps are a fading genre—one that over the years provided work for such a diverse group of actors and incredibly talented behind-the-scenes people like our shows' creators and writers! Together, we were able to provide hours of entertainment for generations of fans, and for that, I will be forever grateful.

It's possible that I will never work in daytime again, but I will work! I just feel so blessed to have been able to bookend my daytime career playing Echo DiSavoy once again on the last remaining soap opera filmed in New York! Like so many of you, I am saddened to see the era of daytime dramas draw to a close, but hey, that's showbiz, right? All good things must come to an end. Without endings, there can be no new beginnings.

So as I type the final words of my memoir, I am left with one singular thought—one that has been on my mind since my last days at *Guiding Light*: How many out-of-work soap opera stars does it take to start their own network. . . ? Hmmmm?

I'm just sayin'!

ACKNOWLEDGMENTS

The notion of writing a book about one's memories and making it interesting enough for other people to want to read could be construed as narcissistic. However, when you're writing about so many years on a show rich with history and pride, people tend to want to know about it. So I feel the need to acknowledge the people who encouraged me to put my thoughts and memories on paper for others to share. . . .

To my kin, specifically Bob Witzel (my sister's husband); Kelly and Nathan Nascimento; Jamie and Glen Harrington; Ralph Sr. and Julia Weary; Jay and Linda Bricker; Abigail and Gary Winestrap; Julie Mueller; Ralph Jr. and Lynn Weary.

No one can have memories without special friendships, so thanks to my friends Ava and Mike Zebrowski; Terri and Bill Heyman; Shelli and Alex Miller; the entire Colatti family, Ray, Barbs, Ray Jr., Tina, Austin and especially my little "tweeter," Adrienne; Nancy and Sterling Swann; Grace and Allen Suddeth; Cathy and Garrett Girvan; Will and Taryn Calhoun; Karen Shehey; and Ed Iannicone.

Thanks to those who so graciously helped me acquire photos that I wanted to use: Alan Locher (I love you); Sue Coflin and

Viki Thompson; Michelle Parkington; Gabby Winkel; Bryan Beckley; Susan Savage; and Joanna Bradford.

My gratitude to ABC and Frank Valentini, who saw fit to resurrect my character of Echo on *One Life to Live* in a timely manner to help my daytime story come full circle for this book!

Big sloppy kisses to my agent, Marnie Sparer, who introduced me to my new "book agent," Jim Stein, who listened to my story pitch and convinced me that it would make a wonderful book and then introduced me to all the great folks at New American Library, starting with the oh so patient Tracy Bernstein, who then put me in touch with several possible cowriters, one of whom I met. I met with only one because after reading her résumé, I knew it would be a match made in heaven. . . . The incomparable (at least in my eyes!) Laura Morton.

When I first met with Laura in L.A., I instantly felt a connection to her. We shared so many of the same interests, and most important, she had a wicked sense of humor, which I knew I wanted if we were going to be spending a great deal of time together. Laura became my therapist as she listened to me vent my anger about *Guiding Light*'s demise, handing me tissues and water when I became overly emotional! With her support I was able to get through the "darkness" so I could find "my light" again. Thank you so much, Laura, for guiding me through this wonderful journey and hearing my voice!

I couldn't finish these thank-yous without saving the best for last. . . .

I have been blessed with the most devoted, loving, funny and heartbreakingly incredible fans! You have given me such joy over these many years and your honest criticism of my work was always so welcomed! You never held back and always let me know what you were feeling about Reva and her escapades. Listening to you at events where I actually got to speak to you or just reading your cards and letters of support gave me the strength to "keep on truckin'" even when I was hating my job! It was you who kept me going!

My final acknowledgment is reserved for my *Guiding Light* family. Thank you to everyone I ever had the pleasure of working with, whether on-camera or off. All of the people who passed through those hallowed halls know that what we shared was something special! We made history together and a lifetime of memories. I miss you all so much!